A Distinctive Setting
for Your House

By Alice Upham Smith

A Distinctive Setting for Your House
Trees in the Winter Landscape
Patios, Terraces, Decks and Roof Gardens

A Distinctive Setting for Your House

LANDSCAPING TO ENHANCE
A HOUSE'S STYLE AND
MAKE THE MOST OF ITS SITE

Alice Upham Smith, l.a.

DOUBLEDAY & COMPANY, INC.
GARDEN CITY, NEW YORK

To my sisters
Janeway and Elizabeth

ISBN: 0-385-01178-4
Library of Congress Catalog Card Number 72–84944
Copyright © 1973 by Alice Upham Smith
All Rights Reserved
Printed in the United States of America
First Edition

Contents

Following page 88:

ONE

Settings for Traditional Houses

Houses and their settings are part of our cultural heritage. In many towns and suburbs you can see how we have copied the beautiful proportions and decorative detail of the homes built by the first colonists from the East Coast to the West and adapted them to our way of life today. We have not only enriched our lives by copying from the timeless quality of those homes, but in many communities from Sag Harbor, Long Island, to Monterey, California, people are lovingly restoring old houses for present-day living.

The style of planting that was done around those original houses is also worth copying, if you wish the setting of your house to be as authentic as the architecture. We have come to associate certain plants with the architecture of each part of the country. New England brings to mind white houses under towering Elms or Sugar Maples, planted by long-ago brides and grooms, and stone walls, picket fences, Rose vines, and Lilacs. Boxwood, Magnolias, Azaleas, and Jasmine make us think of gracious southern homes, while the silvery gray of desert-loving plants, bright colors, and plants in containers represent the Southwest.

Not only does copying the original style of planting add to the authenticity and distinction of a house, it is practical for modern living. The early colonists had many of the same problems in gardening that we have today. They were busy people, therefore any planting had to be easy to keep. Water was scarce: it had to be

A typical New England colonial farmhouse with its bride and groom trees in front. Hackberry or Maple would be a good replacement for Elms today.

Fitch House, Sturbridge Village, 1737. A salt box with an ell at the back. Lilacs and Smokebush soften the corners. Flowers line the dry stone wall and picket fence enclosing the area around the house. *Old Sturbridge Village*

hauled from a well. Houses in town were close together and close to the street for safety and convenience rather than lack of space. Shrubs had to fit the environment. The colonists tried the well-loved shrubs and flowers they had brought with them as slips and seeds and looked about them for native trees and shrubs that did well in each locality. They adapted these to their new way of living, and their plantings were given the highly individual look we admire today.

Fortunately many of the earliest homes are still standing or have been restored at such places as Colonial Williamsburg, Virginia, Old Sturbridge Village in Massachusetts, and the Territorial Capital in Little Rock, Arkansas, to mention a few. Private homes are open on special garden tours all over the United States. Here you can see the original and distinctive styles of foundation planting.

NEW ENGLAND COLONIAL

The Cape Cod style of house with its many variations is one of the most popular house designs in the United States. The first Cape Cod houses were one or one and a half stories high with a chimney in the center. Usually the front door was centered with two windows on each side. Sometimes the builder had to start with half a house, leaving the door and chimney at one end. It was easy to add wings and ells as needed. Rooms were also added by extending the roof down lower at the back. This type of house was called a salt box.

Planting in front of Cape Cod houses was simple. There were low plants by the front doorstep, which was often made of a slab of granite, and flowering shrubs, perhaps Lilacs, at the corners of the house. Sometimes there were Roses around the doorway.

Today we have a much larger variety of evergreens and shrubs to choose from, but to make the planting in front of a Cape Cod house distinctive it should be restrained. These little houses hug the ground. They are well proportioned and have simple yet

No matter what the size, the same simple planting suits a New England colonial house.

Climbing Roses decorate but do not obscure the simple lines of the Cape Cod house. *Taloumis*

dignified details. Do not smother them in a sea of planting. Tie the house to the ground by letting the foundation show in places. Call attention to the door with low evergreens or vines, and soften the corners with shrubs. Use a border of low ground cover along the foundation to save trimming grass. A fence around the front lawn with Roses, Hollyhocks, and other flowers would also be typical. The same restrained style of planting goes with large two- or three-story New England colonial houses.

The Ward House in Salem, Mass., built in 1684 in the English Gothic or Tudor style, has a charming and useful herb and flower garden along a path leading to the back door. *Author*

ENGLISH TUDOR OR ENGLISH COTTAGE

Some of the very earliest homes in New England copied the Tudor or English cottage style of architecture and planting. Those houses had many gables, ornate pilastered chimneys, and small diamond-paned windows. The colonists covered the traditional exposed beam and plaster construction with clapboards for greater warmth, but today we let them show again. In front of or at the side of their houses they planted dooryard gardens similar to the cottage gardens

How nice to be welcomed at the side door of a country home in Maine by a colorful bed of flowers. *Ivan Flye*

they had left behind. These delightful gardens, large or small, were colorful mixtures of herbs and flowers. The herbs were used for cooking, medicine, and fragrance. Today we are taking a renewed interest in herbs, especially for cooking. Paths of gravel or brick, bordered by low hedges, led from the front or side door to a gate in the fence by the road. Sundials and beehives were popular. There was often a fruit tree and a Rosebush or vine. Sometimes the dooryard gardens were simple, just borders along a path, at other times they copied the popular knot patterns of Elizabethan gardens

7

A knot garden in Massachusetts outlined in hardy Iberis and Boxwood with gravel and wood chips in the centers of the knots. The beautiful armillary in the center of the design is a typical Elizabethan ornament. *Taloumis*

Designs for small knot gardens.

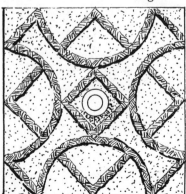

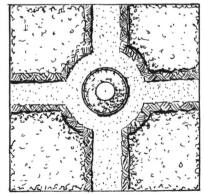

Sheltered on two sides of the house, this dooryard herb garden is convenient to the kitchen. The dark red leaves of the Purple Plum are a vivid contrast to the subdued grays and greens of the herbs. *Taloumis*

with herbs in gray and green designs bright with flowers or colored gravel in the centers. Although this type of gardening looks complicated, it is easy to maintain once it has been constructed.

There were also informal dooryard gardens with pavings of flat stones and masses of low-growing flowers in the spaces between. These charming gardens were popular in front of Cape Cod houses also. White picket fences, rail fences, or stone walls protected them from the road.

The Elizabethan cottage style of architecture was not symmetrical. The building details were heavier and the gables and chimneys more prominent, therefore the planting was thicker, larger in scale, and more informal to balance it. Oaks, Yew, and Holly are the plants you usually associate with English houses. You can mix perennials in masses with shrubs in borders, and plant vines on the walls.

The quaint charm of English Tudor is set off by informal plantings of evergreens, vines, a clipped hedge with topiary balls, and a rugged Oak tree.

Passers-by always admire this quaint little Tudor cottage and its charming informal dooryard planting of vines and perennials. *Bob Ghio*

As the colonies became more prosperous, elegant architectural details were added to houses in the classical ornamentation of the Georgian style. There were wrought-iron railings, pedimented doorways, pilasters, and pillars. In the North, houses were of wood painted white. In the Tidewater region of Virginia, wealthy planters built rectangular brick houses with steep roofs pierced with dormers and end chimneys with sloped weatherings and offsets. Boxwood was a favorite plant for foundation planting. Its fine texture and glossy leaves look so well against brick walls. Boxwood is very slow-growing, so that you can easily control the size of the shrubs and keep them in scale with the house.

Plantings and gardens around the early Virginia homes before the Revolutionary War followed the orderly designs of the Dutch gardens made so popular in England by William and Mary. Tulips and other bulbs kept well on long ocean voyages, so the Box-bordered beds in the gardens were filled with gay colors. Evergreens clipped in topiary style were used for accents. The native Flowering Dogwood, Redbud, Holly, and Magnolia made harmonious plantings around southern homes. Large trees such as Tulip Poplar, Sycamore, Catalpa, Southern Red Oak, Elm, Maple, and Locust framed the houses, sometimes in long avenues leading up to the entrance or on lawns in front of the houses.

Thomas Jefferson preferred the Palladian or Roman form of classical architecture rather than the English Georgian, but he did not stray far from balance and symmetry in house design. In his gardens he liked circular flower beds and winding paths with flowers along the borders. The balanced porticoes of the Palladian style made plantings at the corners unsuitable. Plantings in front of this style of house depend on emphasis on either side of the porticoes.

A simple planting of Boxwood sets off this elegant house. Georgian houses in Tidewater Virginia had steep roofs pierced by dormers and end chimneys. *Colonial Williamsburg; John Crane photo*

Balanced and dignified planting suits a Georgian home in Minneapolis, Minn. *H. H. Livingston, Architect. Courtesy Cabot Stains; Morton and Peel photo*

No corner plantings should obscure the balanced porticoes of a Palladian house. Boxwood or Yew would make an ideal planting.

A Boxwood-lined bulb garden at the side of this Williamsburg house makes looking through the fence a pleasure. *Colonial Williamsburg*

A picket fence repeats the long parallel lines of the gambrel roof of this Dutch colonial house with pleasing effect. *Drawing-photo courtesy Scholz Homes*

DUTCH COLONIAL

Although English architecture and gardening had the greatest influence on building and landscaping along the eastern seaboard, the Dutch also left a legacy which we still copy.

The very earliest stone and brick houses with the steep roofs that the Dutch settlers built are not what we think of as Dutch colonial today. These are the delightful wooden-shuttered houses often with a gambrel roof and dormers, which were built by the Dutch descendants after the colony became English. Stone was abundantly available, and they built sturdy houses of stone with gables of wood and chimneys smoothly set into the ends of the house. Sometimes the roof projected beyond the building to protect the masonry walls and, with columns to support it, became a veranda.

Lacy-leaved yet rugged Locusts are the right frame for a Dutch colonial house. A planting of low ground cover or a dwarf hedge lines the veranda.

There is very little record of the early Dutch planting, but the restoration of the Van Cortlandt estate gives some idea. Locust was the tree most often planted around the houses in the Hudson Valley, and somehow its delicate foliage and strong trunk seem to go with the massive feeling of the masonry houses. Many well-loved Lilacs still live around old foundations. The texture of Lilacs both in summer and when the leaves are gone make them good plants to soften the corners of a sturdy house. The Winged Euonymus, Forsythia, and Regel's Privet would also be good deciduous shrubs for corner planting. Do not break the long line of a veranda with shrubs. Keep the planting in a parallel line and low. Fences or stone walls also help to repeat the long lines of the gambrel roof. Fruit trees and flowers planted in borders along vegetable gardens were also popular.

Large trees and simple but dense-textured planting looks right against the massive stone walls of a Pennsylvania Dutch house.

PENNSYLVANIA DUTCH

The Dutch also settled in Delaware, the southern part of New Jersey, and Pennsylvania along with the Swedish and English who came by way of Holland. The English, many of them Quakers, brought with them from their homeland a love of masonry houses. There was abundant field stone and both the Dutch and English used the rough stone laid in mortar or homemade bricks to build sturdy farmhouses and barns with massive walls. Sometimes the walls were covered over with white plaster. The details of the doors and windows were simple. Shutters, if any, were apt to be of solid wood. You can see where wings were added and additions made as families grew. Many of these old houses in Bucks and Chester counties in Pennsylvania have been lovingly restored and can be seen in all their beauty today.

Such houses had strong character. Framed by the magnificent hardwood trees indigenous to that part of the country, they fitted into the rich farming landscape as though they had grown there, becoming mellower as the years went by. Boxwood and Holly with their dense masses of evergreen leaves made a bold contrast to the forthright simplicity of the stone walls, yet did not cover the entire foundation. Any planting around the base of such a house should be simple and still massive enough to show up against the walls and compete with the character of the building. Any delicate or wishy-washy plant would look lost. Yew would be an excellent choice, and the bold texture of Rhododendron would show up well. Large trees such as Sugar Maple, Beech, Red or White Oak, White Ash, or Sycamore would be right for the lawn.

Stone retaining walls were prevalent along terraces in front of the houses. Trellises and arbors, abloom with Roses, Trumpet Creeper, and heavy with grapes, often led from the kitchen door to herb and flower gardens, in simple geometrical forms suitable for the country, or to vegetable gardens and orchards.

FRENCH PROVINCIAL

In the new world of Canada the French were more noted for exploring than as settlers. The houses around Montreal and Quebec copied Norman cottages and farmhouses, with very steep roofs, useful for shedding snow, and dormer windows. Windows were few and small with wooden shutters. Pictures of houses still standing show a bare and bleak landscape with no planting at all. Probably this was due to the severity of the winter climate and the fear of Indian attacks. The Château de Ramezay in Montreal had Lombardy Poplars in front. Dovecots and sundials were often found.

As the French explored and settled the Mississippi Valley, they began building the same type of houses they had had in Canada, but they stretched out the roofs over wide verandas for shade. Since there was much less snow, roofs did not have to be so steep,

A pioneer cabin.

and two-story houses with verandas on each story were common. For siding they used logs with mud or mortar in between unless there was a sawmill nearby to supply boards. The Swedes were the ones who perfected the log cabin technique of notching logs to make them fit neatly at the corners.

Chimneys on these houses were on the outside. Sometimes in the South the center hall was left open at each end to catch the breezes and was called a "dogtrot." So a type of pioneer architecture evolved in a functional way that fitted its time and place. Split-rail fences kept livestock out of the housewives' native shrubs, wild flowers, and kitchen garden, and forest trees that were not always straight shaded the cabin.

A New Orleans house in the Garden District. *G. E. Arnold*

In New Orleans the settlers found the ground too wet and the water table too high for houses level with the ground. After some years they raised the suburban houses on brick foundations made of timber frames filled with bricks. Plantation houses were often two stories high with pillared verandas.

In 1762 Louis XV ceded Louisiana to Spain. The Spanish did not drive the French out but mixed with them. It was during this period that the houses we think of as typical of New Orleans were built. For privacy from muddy streets and relief from the heat, the homes were built around courtyards with a carriage entrance from the street. Steps led up from the courtyard to living rooms on the second floor with all the rooms opening off balconies

The Norman French provincial house has a steep roof with dormers. *Author*

which overlooked courtyard gardens. There was the sound of splashing fountains, the fragrance of flowers and exotic foliage. There were also narrow balconies along the street with French windows opening to the floor and louvered shutters. The Spanish introduced beautiful wrought-iron balcony railings and grilles for doors in elaborate designs. When the Yankee industrialists developed cast iron, New Orleans was soon hung with lacy balconies.

Gardens in France during the colonization period were very formal. All hedges were clipped, the trees were pleached, and flowers were set out in beds, with borders of low hedges making orna-

French-style house with a mansard roof and a formal forecourt in front.

mental geometrical arrangements called parterres. Sometimes the parterres were made of ribbons of evergreens on gravel. Statuary was important. These gardens suited the elegant details of the houses. They still look best with the type of house we think of as French provincial. There are really several styles of French provincial: the Norman French with its steep roof, the New Orleans type with ornamental ironwork, and the house with a mansard roof. Mansard was a French architect who developed a roof with two pitches, the lower pitch being much steeper than the upper one. Today this type of roof has become very popular again.

You can see the influence of French garden design at the restored Rosedown plantation in Louisiana. There are the formal parterres edged with Boxwood and statuary brought over from France. The warm moist air and the lush growth of the magnificent trees, along with the profusion of flowering shrubs such as Gardenias, Azaleas, Roses, Butterfly Bushes, and Hydrangeas, soften the severity of the formal design and produce an effect that is typical of southern American gardens.

The Llambias house in St. Augustine, Fla., has a secluded garden at the back shut off from the road by a wall and gate. *Courtesy St. Augustine Historical Society*

SPANISH PROVINCIAL

Said to be the oldest house in America still standing, the Llambias house in St. Augustine, Florida, shows the influence of Spanish settlers. The Mediterranean style of architecture took kindly to the tropical climate of Florida and the Gulf Coast. Overhanging balconies or verandas on the second floor shaded windows from the intense sunshine and allowed access to the outdoors from each room. A gate let cooling air into the private patio garden, not only reminiscent of home but a protection against the wilderness outside. A well in the center of a paved area took the place of the usual fountain found in the Moorish gardens of Spain. A pergola covered with vines made a shady passageway from the arched loggia of

Adobe style of architecture.

the house to the well. The white walls of the Llambias house are typical of houses in hot climates where light colors reflect heat and help to keep the houses cool. White is also a brilliant foil for the large leaves of tropical foliage and the brilliant hues of flowers and vines.

In the Southwest, Spanish priests designed the first buildings built by Indian converts. They planned for a patio or central courtyard with a fountain or pool in the center and plants in pots clustered around it. This type of garden fitted in with the hot, dry climate very well. There were verandas on three sides to serve as corridors and shade the windows and doors. If there was a second floor the staircase was also on the outside. The heavy doors were beautifully carved. The Indians taught the Spanish how to build adobe walls three feet thick to keep out the heat. This was a truly indigenous building style copied after the pueblo dwelling, and it was very functional. There were a few small windows. Heavy poles or beams for holding up the ceiling projected through the walls, making a shadow pattern on the plain surfaces of the walls. At first the roofs were thatched, later the thatch was replaced with

Casa de Castro, a typical Monterey home.

tiles like the red tiles of Spain. Outside the houses there were orchards, vineyards, and large vegetable gardens.

The governor's palace in Santa Fe, New Mexico, is a picturesque example of early Spanish colonial architecture. Here the patio is paved in elaborate patterns of pebbles. There is a raised octagonal pool in the center.

Monterey was a most important seaport when California was a colony of Spain. The English who came there to settle made their mark on the Spanish style of house. They followed the basic Monterey form of building with adobe walls and flat-pitched red-tile roofs with wide overhangs to shade windows and doors, but they were carpenters and shipbuilders, so they added wood trim. Often they brought doors, windows, and moldings with them on ship-board. They taught the Spaniards to put stairways inside. The gar-

The House of the Blue Gate in Monterey, Cal., built in 1830. *Courtesy Monterey Chamber of Commerce*

dens around these houses had a distinctly Mediterranean look of formality with clipped hedges of Boxwood and Yew much relieved by the more profuse and softer foliage of Lemons, Palms, and Figs, and brightened by the exuberant colors of Mexican and California flowers in pots clustered about fountains or verandas.

The Monterey adobe house has influenced the modern ranch-style house. It was a functional house for California, combining indoor and outdoor living. Now air conditioning and modern building practices make ranch-style houses even more livable. The basic design and details stemming from the Spanish heritage make new homes look as though they belonged in their settings.

The American Revolution brought a cultural as well as a political liberation. There was a desire to be done with the influence of England and a will to be proudly American.

The competition for the design of the national Capitol stimulated the growth of a distinctly American type of architecture. Led by Washington and Jefferson, who were profoundly influenced by Greek architecture and the grandeur of Rome, designers took up the classic forms. For the first time there were professional American architects, and although they used the Greek architectural orders with their columns, porticoes, and pediments as their inspiration, their work was creative and fluid. The decoration may have been Greek, but in all other ways the buildings were American.

All over the country there was a great interest in fine arts. Growing towns demanded a huge quantity of buildings. Imposing and beautiful state capitols, churches, banks, and custom houses were built from the eastern seaboard to the Mississippi Valley and beyond. There was a sense of planned beauty and composition that made the homes and towns of that period harmonious and distinguished, whether they developed under the spreading 'Elms and Maples along quiet New England streets or among the large trees of new middle western towns in Ohio, or at the end of avenues of Live Oaks on southern plantations. Small houses and large mansions all benefited from careful designing in their proportions and the details around windows and doors. It would be a crime to cover up such beauty with heavy planting, and photos show a very restrained use of shrubbery, if any, around the foundations of the houses and public buildings. The designs were formal, so any planting had to follow in feeling. That does not mean that all shrubs had to be clipped, but it does mean that they were not picturesque or irregular.

In time correctness became such a criterion that the vitality of the revival was doomed. People began to tire of the classic Greek style. More and more Americans were traveling in Europe and

26

A house in Louisville, Ky., with beautiful Greek Revival details. *Johnston*

bringing back a new knowledge and appreciation of Renaissance and Baroque architecture. There was greater wealth and a desire for ostentation in home design.

A renovated Victorian cottage. *Bob Ghio*

VICTORIAN GOTHIC

Gothic romances made people want castles. Atmosphere and effect became all-important. It was fashionable to be picturesque, and the easiest way was to pile Gothic elaboration on houses, using unsuitable material to imitate more expensive ornament.

In 1850 Andrew Jackson Downing, the first American landscape architect, wrote a book, *The Architecture of Country Houses*, describing his philosophy of the ideal American way of life and showing plans for the building of farmhouses, cottages, and country houses or villas. He called his style Rural Gothic, and his books had a profound impression on the buildings and gardens of the late nineteenth century. He liked irregular plans with porches, bal-

28

Common Late Victorian.

Same house with a smaller porch, grading to raise the level along the foundation, and planting to make the house look wider.

conies, bay windows, and turrets, yet he insisted that small houses be simple and straightforward in design, using wood boldly in wide eaves and hoods over doors and windows. He often used large brackets to hold up the eaves. For larger houses, ornamentation was more elaborate, with many porches, balustrades, and fancy verge boards outlining eaves. These were made of heavy planks carved in elaborate designs.

He placed his houses among groups of fine trees. He felt that vines were the perfect adornment. "A wealth of bower and vine makes a house bewitchingly rural," he said. The vines he recommended to gardeners of his day were: Virginia Creeper, Chinese Wisteria, Climbing Roses, Japanese Honeysuckle, Trumpet Honeysuckle, Crape and Hop, with hardy English Ivy for brick or stone.

Later Victorian gardens carried sentimentality and naturalness to the extreme. Walks meandered. There were streams and pools with fountains, and round, crescent- or star-shaped beds in the lawns, filled with Cannas, Coleus, Salvia, and Geraniums.

Downing repeatedly warned his readers against an excess of decoration. He would have been horrified to see what happened when scroll sawwork was made possible by machinery and applied as decoration to the cheap housing of an expanding country. Houses became overloaded with gingerbread and what he called cocked-hat roofs. We are sometimes apt to shudder ourselves when we see Late Victorian mansions. However, stripped of their trimmings inside and out, many make comfortable homes.

Another development that overtook the Victorian house was hot-air heat. The houses had to be raised on high foundations to get headroom in the cellars for the big pipes, and then the ugly foundations had to be covered on the outside. So foundation planting came into style, with houses seeming to float in billows of *Spirea vanhouttei.*

This Late Victorian style can be improved through simplification and modern landscaping. Even Andrew Jackson Downing would feel better about them then.

A Japanese-style house in a setting like that of the Katsura villa.

JAPANESE

On the West Coast especially, you find an awareness of the Orient and a selective appreciation of the Japanese design of houses and gardens adapted to an American point of view.

Japanese houses and gardens are deceptively simple, yet it takes an expert to plan them. They are serene and understated, depending on form rather than color for their beauty.

The Japanese have a great appreciation of the constant patterns of earth, water, and plants. There are always things to lead the eye to link the house and garden, such as low eaves, overhanging tree branches that frame the house, or walks and rocks parallel to the walls, so that the house seems to grow from the landscape.

The courtyard of a Japanese-style house in Los Angeles. *Dorman and Associates, Architects. Geo. de Genero; photo courtesy Cabot Stains*

Their houses and environment are fused into entities. They have a positive genius for solving the problems of overcrowding and not enough privacy, making quiet places for contemplation and refreshment of the spirit. All these are aspects of gardening we are coming to value more and more.

The Japanese make use of natural materials: bamboo and reed for fencing, pebbles and rocks for paving, and gravel for mulching. There are no geometrically planned lawn areas or prim edgings. All is carefully planned to re-create, in miniature, natural scenes. Japanese gardeners rely on suggesting space where it is limited. Paths narrow as they go away from you or disappear around a rock or bush. They go over water, climb mounds, and descend. Seven or eight bamboo stalks close to a house suggest a thicket, as you look through them, and hide another house close by.

By judicious pruning and training, trees are turned into triumphs of artistry. Everywhere you look there is something lovely to contemplate.

There are books on Japanese gardening that will be helpful if you want to try that kind of a garden and there is no expert nearby. An excellent one is *Landscape Gardening in Japan,* by Josiah Conder, Dover Publications. This book goes into complete detail with many drawings, lists of plants, and pictures.

Chinese gardening is a less stylized, more natural art in which all growing things are allowed to follow their own growth habits instead of being trained. The Chinese do not arrange stones to compose pictures but enjoy them as nature made them. Here again you need someone who has a talent for that type of gardening to plan one that is authentic in feeling.

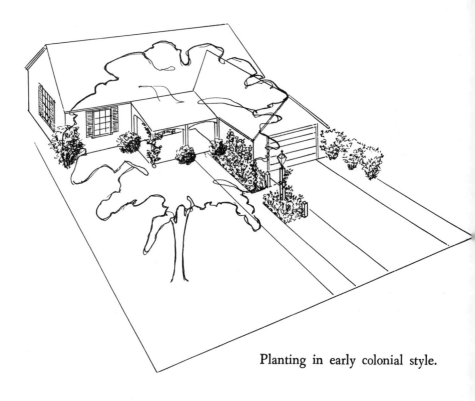

Planting in early colonial style.

Applying Traditional Designs of Planting to Plain Houses

Since each traditional style of house had plantings peculiar to its customs and region, you can give any house without traditional architectural features a distinctive setting by using the special plantings that suit your taste.

If you prefer the warm charm of early colonial, add a picket fence, with a lamp and a border of old-fashioned flowers, along the walk by the side of the garage. Vines on the fence and pillars by the front door add gracious color. Flowering shrubs at the corners and a spreading tree on the lawn finish the correct details.

A more precise and clipped planting goes with the elegance of French provincial. Outline the foundation with a low curving hedge filled in with ground cover, and use clipped evergreens

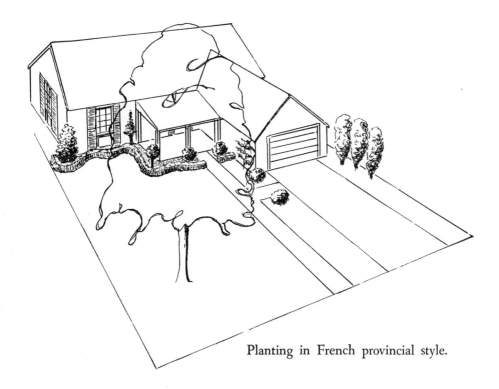

Planting in French provincial style.

for accent. Train a plant in an espalier against the garage wall. Use a trim, rounded tree such as a Little Leaf Linden on the front lawn and small columnar trees along the driveway.

For a Spanish style try a small fountain with a jet of water set into a square of gravel or ground cover in front of the veranda. Pots of flowers emphasize the front entrance and hang colorfully against the garage wall. A dark green Cypress, some Cacti, and a multiple-trunked tree all add to the right atmosphere.

For those who would rather be up to date, a modern planting provides a different look. Use the various textures of paving, gravel mulch, and ground cover to make patterns around the front entrance. A vine against the garage wall makes another pattern, and a tree with several trunks leads the eye over from the prominent garage. Several trees on the front lawn are informal.

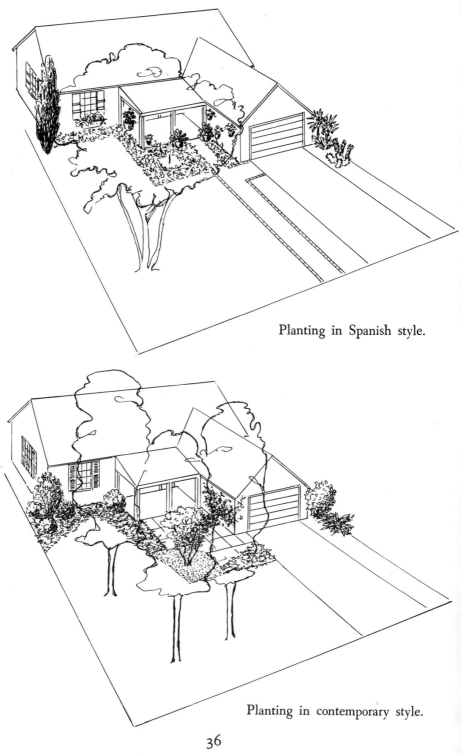

Planting in Spanish style.

Planting in contemporary style.

36

TWO

Suburban Houses

When the Victorian Gothic fever had run its course and people were tired of showy trim and turreted mansions, they were urged to turn back to our own pre-Revolutionary architecture for inspiration. Those basic styles became standard parts of the scene in the twentieth century with here and there some unusual house planned by an architect with the flair of Frank Lloyd Wright.

Unfortunately landscaping around the houses clung to foundation planting monotonously the same, although fads in plants came and went. When automobiles became numerous, owners built garages as separate buildings at the back of the property. Later they became a part of the house itself, which made them prominent parts of the scene in front.

Houses and gardens changed considerably after World War II. Economy forced the building of smaller, simpler houses, usually one story high. In warm climates there were carports instead of garages. In an effort to make the houses seem larger inside, builders put picture windows in the living rooms. In most cases this was in the front of the house facing an uninteresting street. Either the owners lived in what looked like a store window or pulled the curtains shut to keep out the sun and the gazes of passers-by, thus defeating the purpose of the windows. Many split-level houses made use of a drop in the grade to set the garage low and put some rooms above it up just a few steps from the living area.

There were some improvements in landscaping. There was no need for heavy foundation planting. Sliding doors opened out onto

Have fun with driftwood and rocks. The decoration against a house does not always have to be plants. *Ray Grass*

patios and decks at the back of the house, so that it was easier to enjoy outdoor living.

Builders bought up tracts of land and mass-produced houses, using several changes in floor plans and outside trimming for variety. Usually they bulldozed the land flat, removing every tree and blade of grass in the interests of easier and more economical building. Where land sloped, they often used the same plans with little regard as to how they fitted on the site. Although most of these tract or development houses have little distinctive style, they are good value in living space for the money. Landscaping is one way of giving a standard house a custom-built look. You can have a good-looking house in poor surroundings that detract, or a plain house in a charming setting that makes it a show place. The charm of a house comes from its harmony with its planting and

The curving lines of planting beds turn a slope with hard rock ledges into a charming setting. When the broad-leaved evergreens are in bloom it is very colorful. *Genereux*

layout, and this does not mean that it has to be expensive or elaborate. Sometimes two or three perfect plants are better than a dozen common ones.

At present the trend in building and gardening is toward "doing your own thing" and having fun with it, whether that is lovingly restoring an old house or designing and building your own to fit your needs. There is a greater interest in good design and in improving the environment. This makes much more variety in houses and gardens. Houses are larger again. New building materials and methods add more changes.

Foundation planting as such is out of date. It clutters up the design of the house and makes extra work, besides getting in the way of window washing and painting. A house looks as though it belongs on its site when it sits clearly and cleanly on the ground.

The line of Ivy in front of the veranda decorates but does not obstruct the view of this peaceful secluded garden shaded and cooled by trees. *Molly Adams*

Regard the front lawn area as a total space that you can plan to suit your needs and to beautify the house. Use plants to emphasize good points and cover up poor ones. Low-maintenance gardening is the first consideration. There is very little garden help available and most of it is unskilled. Homeowners are too busy and prefer to use leisure having fun rather than pruning shrubbery or weeding flower beds. The less there is to do to keep the front of the house looking well, the better.

Today we face unique problems in landscaping, among those are the need to learn the effect of pollution on plants and to find those plants that will survive and look well under difficult conditions.

A planter filled with Japanese Holly (*Ilex convexa*) in front of the bay window trims and protects it without covering the foundation. A Euonymus vine softens the planter and a spreading Japanese Yew emphasizes the door. *Genereux*

The Agricultural Research Service of the United States Department of Agriculture is doing research in the Plant Pollution Laboratory at Beltsville, Maryland, to determine species resistant to pollutants. There is a list of pollution-resistant plants in the last section of the book, but it is always a good idea to check with your local nurseryman since conditions vary so much from place to place.

We also have increased levels of noise. Plants can help muffle the sound of nearby lawn mowers, barking dogs, and TV as well as street traffic and planes overhead. Impending power shortages make cooling shade trees necessary to take some of the load off air conditioners. The shade of trees lowers the temperature around a

Outside lighting at night is another safeguard. *General Electric Company*

house about seventeen degrees. If you plant a tree ten feet away from a window it will act as a natural air conditioner, directing a current of air toward the window.

In some parts of the country, prickly bushes under windows would add protection from prowlers. These are all things to consider in planning the setting for your home.

The following sketches and pictures show landscaping solutions to some of the problems of standard house plans. The sketches cannot cover every situation but there should be enough different ideas to illustrate the principles of landscape design in trying to solve your specific problem. In some sketches you can look through the outlines of the trees to see the details of the house. Only the forms of plants are suggested. Lists of plants for each form and various locations are in the last section of the book.

The Prominent Garage

Garages and driveways are important parts of the landscape, but if the garage juts out in front of the house it becomes too prominent and something has to be done to call attention to the rest of the house. Plan a feature to lead the eye toward the walk and front door. In the first example a section of fence with a vine encloses the end of the walk, making a strong visual line leading away from the garage and toward the house. Three flowering trees on the lawn in front of the picture window and toward the corner of the house make a mass of foliage to balance the bulk of the garage as well as providing some privacy for the window.

Land sloping away from the garage to the left makes a stronger treatment necessary. A lamp and several low evergreens make the entrance walk more important, while two pines on the lawn are dramatic enough to make a definite accent. A planter going around the corner of the house adds to the feeling of weight to counteract the visual weight of the garage. Either one of these plans would require little maintenance.

Notice how the curving lines of the planting beds follow the contours and lead the eye away from the garage wing. The Pine in the foreground has been carefully pruned to represent a windswept tree in the oriental style. The ground cover is Purple Winter Creeper (*Euonymus fortunei coloratus*). *Elizabeth Howerton, L.A.; Gretchen Harshbarger photo*

A Long Unbroken Roof Line

The house with a long unbroken roof line and no architectural distinction needs help in two ways. First and most important, it needs the height and varied outlines of trees to break up the line of the roof. Trees work wonders in the landscape, and since it takes awhile for them to reach a size where they show up to advantage, plant them first if there are none around. Trees also make beautiful shadows against the walls. Use several different kinds of trees to get diverse silhouettes.

This type of house needs more than a shrub on either side of the front door for emphasis. One solution would be to offset the

walk so that as you come toward the house you face a handsome specimen evergreen or a plant in a container rather than the door itself. Plant a hedge around the entrance slab and extend it in front of the window to the left of the door. This will give the whole area more interest.

Another way to add interest to the house would be to curve the walk up to the front door, continuing the curve in a wide bed of low shrubs and ground cover around the corner of the house. Tall trees in front of the door and one as an accent in the curving bed are balanced by a tree with a round head on the left. Stepping-stones go through a bed of ground cover and low shrubs to the garage.

Everyone Goes to the Back Door

You probably know of a house where everyone automatically goes to the back door. It seems to be the most convenient and inviting place to go, although the owner may not appreciate it.

The corner lot house above had such a pretty patio opening out from sliding glass doors in back next to the kitchen door that everyone who drove in stopped right there. In order to change the pattern, give the front walk more importance with a circular turn and a flower border, and hide the patio from guests parking in the semicircular driveway. You could add a gate on the walk leading to the patio to make it more private. The strip between the walk and the house is a perfect place for a flower border if it is on

the sunny side. An evergreen and flowering trees between the drive and the street provide privacy for the house.

Even if that house was not on a corner lot, people drove way in to the back and went in the kitchen door. Make it easy for them to park before they get too far, and they will find the walk to the front door inviting and convenient. An evergreen in each of the triangles formed by the diagonal parking makes a dramatic planting and hides the driveway from the neighbors.

Seclusion

There are times when some seclusion would be a help in front, but a fence or boundary planting is out of the question. If there are no trees on the lawn, grade the lawn upward from a low line eight to ten feet out from the house to just beyond the center line of the lawn. Plant shrubs and flowering trees in a curving line along the crest of the mound and slope it gently down to street level. A rise of even two or three feet with shrubs and trees on top gives wonderful privacy. If you do the grading when the house is being built, this is a simple procedure.

A simpler solution for a house with a picture window in front would be to plant three large evergreens or dense trees with low branches, such as Pin Oak, in a wide triangle with the farthest one out at least twenty-five feet, so that light and sunshine can get in the window, but the view is broken from the street.

Split Level

Where there is a change in grade, dropping from the one-story part of a split level to the two-story end, a small amount of filling in front of the entrance will make a level walkway. Curve the bank to emphasize the curve of the walk and make a nice transition. Ground cover inside the curve and on the bank will reduce lawn mowing. Notice how a prominent evergreen tree at the right of the garage helps to balance the large mass of the two-story wing. A tall

shrub or small tree at the left-hand lower corner makes that end seem shorter.

The same split-level house on a lot that slopes toward the street can have quite a different aspect. A walk with easy steps curves among birch trees and ground cover to the front door. The front area has a secluded natural look. Guests who park in the driveway can enter by the side entrance on the porch.

The House That Is Two Stories High at One End

The house that is two stories high at one side and only one on the other is a greater challenge, but the result can be interesting with sculptured banks or retaining walls. Where the ground slopes in two directions, down across the house and also toward the street, curve or angle the retaining walls so that they gradually reduce in height until they finally blend with the slope. Looking out at them from the house the point where the walls and slope meet should not break the smooth flow of the lawn. Two walls, one above the other, make fine easy-to-work-in places for growing flowers and vines.

If you do not want to build walls, grade the lawn in a gradual slope down to the lower level and make a wide planting of shrubs below the porch. The temptation is to hide the exposed foundation on the lower level, but avoid that. Use vines or an espaliered plant or a shrub or small tree with multiple trunks at the lower corner.

When the land in front of this house plan is flat in front, bring the entrance walk in, in a curve to the front of the porch, and have the railing at the side. This will make room for more planting and privacy in front of the window.

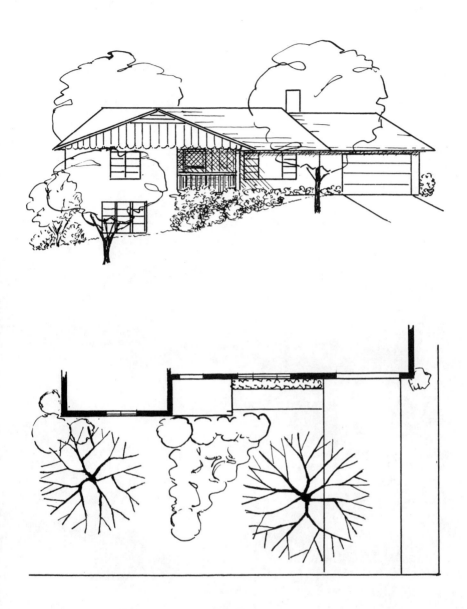

A curving walk with easy steps leads through a rock garden from the lower-floor driveway to the entrance above. The rock garden, house, and wooded area all blend into a natural and beautiful composition. *Molly Adams*

A Formal Two-Story House

A wide straight walk lined with a low hedge makes a gracious entrance to a formal two-story house, and it is the one that is usually seen. Another traditional way of landscaping these houses is to have a semicircular driveway in front of the house, as shown on the next page.

If you wish to build a traditional formal house on property which slopes from one side to another, the plan of approach will have to change to suit the different levels. It must still be formal. Have the garage on a higher level with steps down and a curved planter by the veranda. Run the walk straight across the front to another curved planter on the far side, which maintains the same

level on the left-hand corner, then take the walk down to the street where steps will be necessary. Ground cover on the banks will avoid difficult mowing. Plant trees that will grow large on the front lawn and, where there are walls without windows, plant vines on the house.

When the lawn slopes toward the street and you want a curving driveway, build a retaining wall about a third of the way out from the house to the street, and level the ground in front of the house. Plant low evergreens where the driveway makes banks as it cuts through the wall.

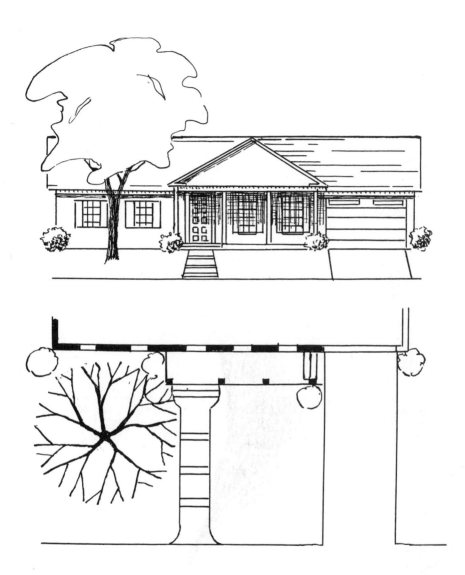

A Formal Design

A house that is formal in design calls for formality in landscaping. This does not mean that every tree must be just so many feet from the front door; there may be beautiful trees already on the site and they will look well where they are. However, the grading and the walks and drives look best if they follow an orderly symmetrical pattern. Ordinarily a straight walk to the front door is correct. If the

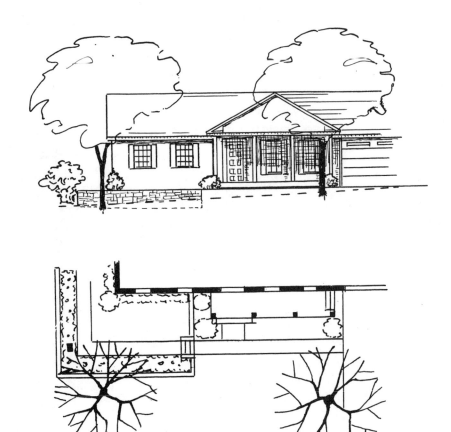

front lawn slopes down to the street, break the walk into a series of double steps, leaving four to five feet between each pair of steps. Depending on your stride, that will make two paces between steps. People are apt to trip if there is only one step at a time. Try to have two even if they have to be five to seven feet apart.

You can have a formal house on sloping land if you fill in, in front of the entrance, to make it level. Use some of the dirt from a cut. Make a sunken garden on the low side. You can have a sheltered flower garden or plant ground cover and evergreens in it. A wall on the outside parallel with the house carries the horizontal line of the entrance grade straight across the house.

The Small House

A very small house needs to have all the feeling of expansion it can achieve. Widen the driveway for a walk and let it lead into a generous front walk. Cut an angle out of the walk to show off a pretty spreading tree in front of the window. Enclose the area next to the carport to make a private patio that can be used in connection with the carport for parties if the car is parked in the drive. A hedge of something like Barberry or Yew along the front of the patio and a similar one at the other end of the house make the house seem longer. It ties the design together. Several trees of varying height break the monotony of the roof line and shade the house.

Two gentle steps down and a deck make an entrance into a multilevel home. The Pines and rocks in front look just right with the natural siding of the house. *California Redwood Association; Julius Shulman photo*

Multilevel House

Too often you see walks leading down from a driveway to some steps going up to a front door. To go down and then up is not only unsightly but senseless. Why not build a deck, leaving room in front of the window for plants? The deck could be large enough to sit on if there is a pleasant view at the front of the house. Or instead of a deck you could build a low retaining wall and fill in between it and the house to make a level place for a walk and some plants. Low evergreens at the end and corner of the deck soften the construction lines. Make the part of the deck at the doorway a minimum of six feet wide. If it is high, use a wood or wrought-iron railing.

Broad gentle steps tie a brick-paved patio to a wooden deck that extends out over the water. The tree was especially chosen and pruned to show its beautiful branch formation. *Edward D. Stone, Jr., L.A.; Photo courtesy American Association of Nurserymen*

A House Fronting on the Water

When there is water, the water side of the house is often the most important with the prettiest setting. With water you need a dock. Make the dock large enough to act as a deck and connect it to the house with easy wide steps to a smaller deck in front of the windows. Frame the house with trees as you see it from the water, and also frame the view from the window looking out over the water. The sun makes a glare on the water, so shade is very welcome. If it is salt water, check with your local nursery to see that all plants can stand salt spray from a storm.

A house on a rocky, sloping shore needs level space around it for living areas. Don't cut down trees. Let them grow though the deck. Have as large a deck as possible and a paved space at the side, so that there will be no lawn to mow. Steps down to the dock or float and a path sloping through the rocks and undergrowth make access to the water easy. Plant some attractive native shrubs and wild flowers to add to those already on the site, and forget garden chores.

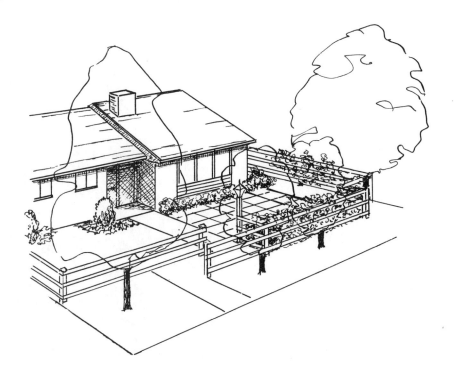

The House with a Patio in Front

Sometimes the best view or the sunniest spot is at the front of
the house. That would make an ideal spot for an outdoor living area
if only there was some privacy. Fencing provides the most privacy
and takes up the least space. If you bring the entrance into the yard
at right angles to the walk, it makes the whole area more secluded
right at the start with no need for a gate. A fence makes a pleasing
background for vines or flowers. Set the fence back from the lot line
about six feet so that it will not look too forbidding to passers-by
and so that there will be room for several trees for height and shade.

A patio curving around a large shade tree would be pretty with a curving walk ending at a gate and perhaps two steps at the street. Steppingstones going over to the patio are more informal than a walk. Fill in the space between the steppingstones and the house with ground cover to make a pattern on the ground and eliminate some lawn mowing. A bench around the tree would be attractive. Fill in the space behind the tree with shrubs. A thick planting of shrubs around the edge makes it really private for outdoor living.

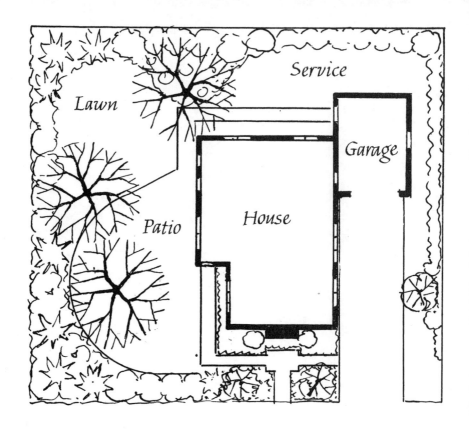

The House with the Narrow End Facing the Street

A house takes up less room if the narrow side faces the street. This allows a nice space for a private living area at the side. The plan shows an entrance walk centering on the chimney with one section going to the driveway and one around the house to the left through the patio to the front door. You can combine the walk paving with the patio paving or make a special design in the paving to designate the walk. Large evergreens and shrubs along the property line shield the area from neighboring houses. The planting against the house is low except for an espaliered plant or vine against the chimney.

66

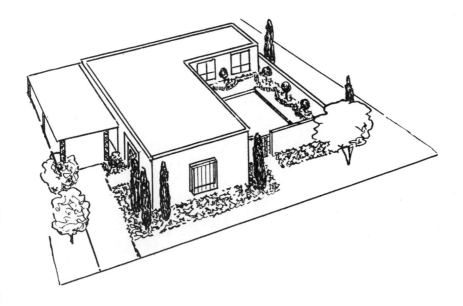

An L-shaped house with its narrow end facing the street has an ideal spot for a walled-in swimming pool. The front door is on the opposite side of the house by the carport. Three stately Cypress trees in a wide bed of low prostrate Juniper give the entrance importance. The Juniper continues along the front of the house and there is one Cypress at the opposite side. No leafy tree should overhang the pool, but one on the outside of the wall contrasts with the dramatic upright shape of the Cypress. To relieve all the straight lines, make a scalloped border of a low shrubby perennial such as Teucrium or Santolina to outline the planting around the pool.

THREE

Details Make a Difference at the Doorway

Give the small house that starts out looking just like its neighbor some personality by focusing attention on the planting and trim at the front door. You can add country charm, a feeling of elegance, Old World tradition, or modern sophistication by your choice of plants and accessories. Using the various shapes, colors, and textures of shrubs along with simple architectural aids that any homeowner can install, such as shutters, moldings, trellises, or planters, you can get away from stereotyped doorway plantings and have an imaginative and inviting entrance. Good proportion, uncluttered design, and careful workmanship are important to success. The kind of furnishings you like inside should influence your selection of style.

Probably one of the first ideas that comes to mind, and one of the easiest ways to add a different touch, is to frame the door with shutters in a color that contrasts with the siding of the house. Many Cape Cod and other colonial homes with simple doorways had shutters. They usually had a good-sized comfortable doorstep made of a slab of granite or bricks. If you wish to have a colonial-style entrance, then use shutters. Give a small doorstep added weight and importance by adding a low plain planter on either side. Make them of stone, concrete, or brick—whichever matches the existing walk and doorstep. Fill each planter with a handsome specimen evergreen such as Japanese Yew, Arborvitae, or Japanese Holly. Azaleas, where they are hardy, would be colorful in a

The parallel lines of the sidewalk echo the horizontal lines of the door pattern and make a very effective treatment. *William Aplin*

partially shady spot. Let Baltic Ivy soften the edges, or use Geraniums or Begonias to add summer color. Top off the whole arrangement with a charming colonial-style light fixture above the door. Keep the rest of the planting along the foundation very simple or non-existent except for a nice shrub at each corner.

Another way in which to give a simple doorway a custom-built look would be to add a one-inch band of color around the doorframe and then a four-inch molding in the same color as the trim on the

doorframe. The molding you choose at the lumber yard will have a bearing on the style. A plain four-inch board can have the look of a primitive colonial farmhouse if you choose hinges, latches, and lanterns in that style. Train a Rose vine around the door on wires for the right touch. A four-inch board could also be starkly modern with the correct lights and other accessories. Use an espaliered Firethorn on either side or, farther north, geometrically trimmed evergreens.

A modern trellis design at the edge of a planter is heavy enough to support a Wisteria vine. *Molly Adams*

A shaped molding has a more elegant look and calls for more elaborate lamps. The glossy leaves of a Euonymus vine trained up and over the door would be in keeping. The color between the doorframe and molding also changes the decorative accent. Dark glossy colors are rich and dignified, earthy colors more primitive, and bright ones modern. Be sure the band of color does not clash with the color of Rose vines or the orange berries of the Firethorn. Low evergreens on either side of the doorway would help to define the planting. Dwarf Mugho Pine makes a round-shaped plant for a sunny place, while Japanese Yew likes shade. Dwarf Yaupon would do well in the South.

A latticework arbor enclosing a doorway is another way to use softening vines for decoration. This plan is charming and quaint. It seems to belong to a cottage garden with lots of gay flowers and window boxes. The arbor can be just the width of the doorstep or wide enough for seats on either side of the door. Make it rounded or squared off at the top with vines clambering over it to make it a bower. The framework of the trellis is a heavy enough decoration so that you can do without evergreens as accents on either side of the door if you prefer.

For those who enjoy French provincial, wrought-iron grillwork can take the place of a vine. The lacy framework shows off like frosting, especially if it is white against a darker setting. Keep the planting formal. Set it off with plain round light globes for a contrast, and plant broad-leaved evergreens with fairly large leaves. Rhododendrons or Burford Holly would be handsome. So would the bronze winter leaves of Oregon Grape Holly. In colder areas try the deciduous dwarf Cranberry Viburnum.

For a less expensive treatment, the homeowner who is handy

can build a latticework pattern between battens or strips of two-by-two lumber and paint them a color that contrasts with the background. Experiment with an oriental motif and plant shrubs that will grow in a picturesque fashion. Search the nurseries for crooked Scotch Pine. You may get a bargain. Trim Pfitzer Juniper with an oriental cut. Nandina with its Bamboo-like leaves would be good and small Japanese Maples with their lacy red leaves are beautiful. For a large doorway two Red Jade Crabapples would be spectacular.

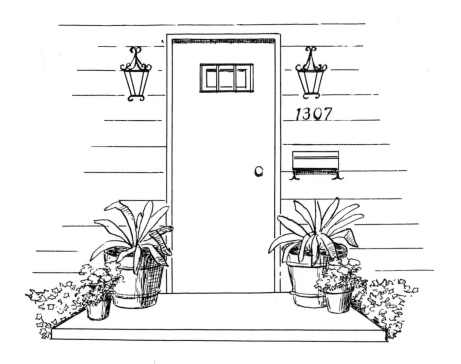

Some plants definitely set a mood and suggest a theme. Yuccas or succulents in heavy earthenware jars seem to call for a Spanish treatment. Paint the door a bright color and add wrought-iron lamps and bars over the door glass. Add a few extra pots of Geraniums, and you will have something different.

If you live in an area where driftwood is abundant, use it to decorate an informal doorway scheme. It is usually more difficult to work out a natural-looking planting than a formal one, but well worth the effort. The soft gray color of driftwood looks at home with the native evergreens, Juniper, Pine, and Hemlock. Place a piece of driftwood in a vertical position and plant Bar Harbor or Blue Rug Juniper at the base. If the house is light in color give the driftwood an evergreen background of an upright Pfitzer.

A Japanese treatment for a modern doorway is striking. The fiberglass roof lets in light but keeps out rain. *William Aplin*

Railings are a good architectural aid for adding individuality to a doorway. In Williamsburg you see wrought-iron railings on front steps of modest homes. They add a touch of elegance. Add shrubs such as Boxwood, Euonymus, or Privet trimmed into formal round or pyramidal shapes. Plant them in tubs painted dark green. Some carriage lamps would help to carry out the picture of elegant formality. For a change have the railing parallel with the doorway and plant a very low hedge in front of it so as not to hide it. Some of the shrubs recommended as edgings in Chapter Five, "Dooryard Gardens," would be helpful.

77

Asymmetrical architecture and a large Pine in front of the door help to set the mood for a natural planting of Rhododendron, Hemlock, and Dwarf Yew. *Genereux*

Every detail of this entrance is elegant. The wrought-iron and brick fence enclosing the paving is in keeping. There are espaliered Yews against the arched recesses. *Genereux*

Wooden railings painted white are also attractive. You can make them of two-by-twos. Even better, you may be able to find some turned balusters from an old house that is being torn down and make an imposing railing of them. It takes only eight or ten. With such a heavy railing add pilasters to frame the door. This would call for a planting of evergreens that are dense in texture as a foil for the railings. Yew and Japanese Holly are dense. In the North use Alpine Currant.

Old houses being dismantled often yield treasures of wood ornaments, perhaps the canopy from a Victorian doorway or some of the gingerbread used for trimming around the eaves. With them use such favorites of the period as Bridal Wreath or Honeysuckle.

Decorative concrete blocks are another idea for railings. They set a completely different and more informal mood. The blocks come in many patterns, and it takes only a few to make a railing. Euonymus and Hydrangea vines look well twining among the openings. Since the blocks are geometrical they combine well with planters. You could use low brick walls one brick thick with openings between the bricks if concrete blocks are not available. There are cement bricks as well as clay bricks.

Architects often use planters as decorative accents on custom-built houses. It is one way of adding a distinctly contemporary look to a house. You can make planters of various shapes and sizes, either all on one level or on several different levels. It is easy to add a brick or stone finish with the veneers that come ready to cement on. Railroad ties make effective planters for a house with natural siding, and large flue tiles are handsome ready-made planters. Offset the walk to the door and make it more interesting.

Good planting alone, if it has pattern enough to be architectural, can give a front door distinction. Instead of the one evergreen on either side of the doorway make a design of several plants trimmed so that they will have the effect of a wall. Accent them with higher forms of the same shrub or use statuary or a flowering tree.

Your front door does more than anything else to project an image, so give it a distinctly personal touch.

Douglas Rucker, Architect. *Richard Gross photo*

FOUR

Distinctive Houses and Distinctive Sites

Sometimes the design of a house is so imaginative and emphatic that it dominates the scene. It is almost like a piece of sculpture and the site should be played down in contrast so that every line of the house stands out crisp and clean. Set it on an open carpet of grass for all to enjoy. If there are large areas of blank wall, place a few trees where they will make elegant or picturesque silhouettes and shadows against the wall and on the lawn.

Reserve any intricate planting for areas around a patio or pool, or in a courtyard where it can be seen intimately.

There are other times when the site is so beautiful or outstanding, or perhaps just difficult to build on, that it determines the way in which the house should be built and the lines of the house. The house should accommodate itself to the site. To fit a house properly to a site so that there are no building scars and to make it look as though it had grown there shows high architectural ability.

The long parallel horizontal lines of an Arizona house fit comfortably into the side of a hill with a backdrop of mountains and a desert foreground. One strong vertical line like a buttress on the low side repeats the line of the mountain behind. The entrance and garage are on the other side of the house. The only garden area is a small rock garden and pool joining a patio where the owners can enjoy their superlative view.

A hilltop provides an eminence for a house. The lines of the house in the next sketch follow the line of the hill from all angles so

Charles E. Cox, Architect. *Jarvis photo*

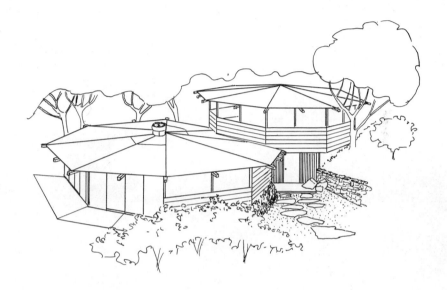

that the house looks like the peak of the hill. There are terraces and decks for level walking spaces around the house, and the garage is comfortably at street level. On a higher level there is a swimming pool.

Instead of having a house one story high at one end and two at the other end, the architect planned the house in this sketch in two octagonal sections in a stair step, so that the upper one has a view over the roof of the lower one, and the lower part has windows opening at ground level. The whole house looks as though it nestles into the side of the hill. There are no landscaping problems at all. The garage is in a separate building.

California Redwood Association. *Geo. Lyon photo*

Cantilevered over a steep cliff, this California house is suited to
its site because it conforms to the over-all contours of the land.
Although the planes of the roof are flat, they have some interest.
The informal planting in the narrow strip in front of the house,
while adding a softening pattern to the blank walls of redwood
siding, does not spoil the lines of the house. The rocks with Juniper
in the foreground are the type of natural landscape you might find
on a cliff.

Let a beautiful tree be the feature that determines the plan.

Take any natural feature into consideration when planning a house and garden. If there is a pond or pool, use it to reflect the house and double the beauty. Running water adds life and movement to a scene. Show off a brook by skillfully featuring waterfalls and building a bridge over a narrow section. Treat rock outcroppings with restraint, letting the natural beauty of the rocks tell their own story.

California Redwood Association. *Morley Baer photo*

1. An inviting doorway to an inner courtyard with plants in containers. *Guy Burgess*

2. Heaths and heathers
at an informal front entrance.
Eleanor Finlayson

3. The beauty of form and color in planting. *Genereux*

4. A tropical setting. PPG *Industries, Inc.*

5. Mobile Home. *Conan*

6. Authors dooryard garden in early Spring.

7. Summer color, carefree geraniums in the sun, elfin impatiens in the shade.

Pan American Seed Co.

Port Royal Plantation, Hilton Head, S.C.; *Ned Brown photo*

A large tree is a priceless asset. If there are any on the property, plan your house to take advantage of them. Let them come up through a deck or in an atrium in the center. Saving a tree is preserving part of the environment. See how cleverly the architect used the multiple trunks of the tree to compliment the lines of the house opposite and frame the door and stained-glass window. It becomes an integral part of the design.

The architect used this sprawling Live Oak (above) to frame a long low house of neutral-colored siding and simple lines. The tree is the dominant feature in the landscape, and the house fits into its setting quietly and beautifully.

89

The author's dooryard garden. No lawn to mow. Flowers to enjoy.

A fence in front encloses a small private garden in front of a picture window, making the room seem larger.

FIVE

Dooryard Gardens for Today's Houses

Dooryard gardens have always been functional as well as charming. They seem to belong to small houses, and since we have a limited amount of space in the average house today and less and less land, dooryard gardens are one answer to adding distinction, beauty, and livability to the front of your home. They add an extra dimension to gardening at the front, making an inviting entryway which seems like an extension of the house, and creating an interesting view from inside. They replace the usual monotonous row of evergreen foundation plants with a personal garden plan that suits the house and owner. When the plantings are moved out from under the windows, you can enjoy them. It makes the rooms inside seem larger, and the house has more privacy.

These little gardens, even the most casual ones of steppingstones and ground cover, have a basic structure of paths and plantings that is interesting even when the flowers are gone. The crisp outline of stones, brick edgings or low hedges, and the patterns of walks shows even under snow, clearly marking the design.

Fences or hedges on the outer border define the garden and protect the plants from anyone cutting across the property. Best of all, dooryard gardens are easy to maintain once they are established. After you have laid out the design, you can choose the type of planting you have time to care for, making it as simple or elaborate as you wish. There is no lawn to mow, only a few weeds once in awhile, and some trimming. Even those chores can be reduced to

A courtyard is an ideal place for a small private dooryard garden. The exposed aggregate paving is in a restful pattern of squares. Tropical plants and a tree provide shade and color. *Edward D. Stone and Associates*

An informal dooryard garden with a path of steppingstones in gravel, very easy to maintain.

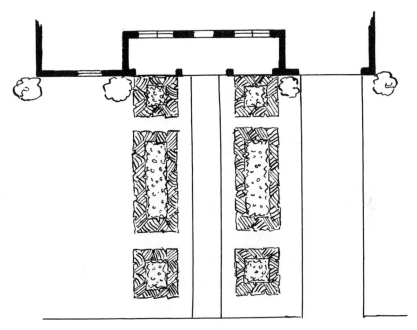

Formal parterres of flowers or Azaleas enclosed by an evergreen hedge.

a minimum by mulching the beds and choosing plants that require little pruning. It means also that you can concentrate flowers in a limited area where you can enjoy them.

Designs vary to harmonize with different styles of architecture from the most up-to-date modern to the most old-fashioned and traditional. Some are very casual and simple in plan; others extremely formal with clipped Boxwood or herb hedges intricately interwoven, with the spaces between filled with bulbs and gay bedding plants. In between are simpler geometrical designs of small beds bisected by paths.

A dooryard garden screens the parking area from the front window.

There is a charm about an old-fashioned dooryard garden that nothing can surpass. Whether they would like to have one or not, most people admire them. Perhaps it is due to the intimate connection to the house and the feeling of being enclosed in a small paradise of color and fragrance. The formal layout of the small beds with their balanced design and neatly edged paths gives a feeling of serenity. There is no stiffness. Clumps and drifts of flowers grow naturally in riots of color.

An old-fashioned dooryard garden in a modern suburban setting. Notice how the enclosure seems to extend the size of the house. Carlton B. Lees, Director of the Massachusetts Horticultural Society, designed the garden for his home. *Horticulture Magazine; Geo. M. Cushing photo*

Another view of Mr. Lees's garden shows the charm of a flower garden in front of a house in contrast to the usual sedate evergreen planting. *Horticulture Magazine; Geo. M. Cushing photo*

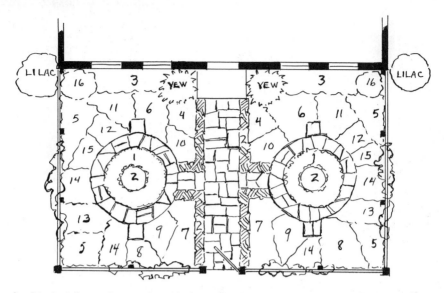

A planting for a dooryard garden: 1. Creeping Phlox. 2. Teucrium or Box-wood. 3. Ajuga. 4. Dianthus. 5. Lavender. 6. Veronica. 7. Heather. 8. *Sedum spectabilis.* 9. Lemon Balm. 10. Marigolds. 11. Campanula. 12. Chives. 13. Artemisia. 14. Beebalm. 15. Sage. 16. Peony.

Originally flowers in cottage dooryard gardens were chosen for fragrance in scenting lotions and soap, and interplanted with herbs for household use and cooking. The concentrated perfumes of Roses, Lilies, Pinks, and Peonies and the aromatic smell of Lavender, Thyme and Mint mingling together on a warm sunny day made a heady fragrance. What a change that would make from our polluted atmosphere!

Tall Stocks or ruffled Hollyhocks along a fence or dwarf Apple or Pear trees trained against a fence or wall add to the quaint charm. Sundials, beehives, or small evergreens cut in topiary forms make cozy accents in scale with the size of the garden.

You can use compositions of foliage plants in restful shades of gray and green or have a garden of green with dramatic accents of sculpture. Here is a place for experimenting with beds of two or three contrasting colors of annuals, changing them from year to year to suit your mood.

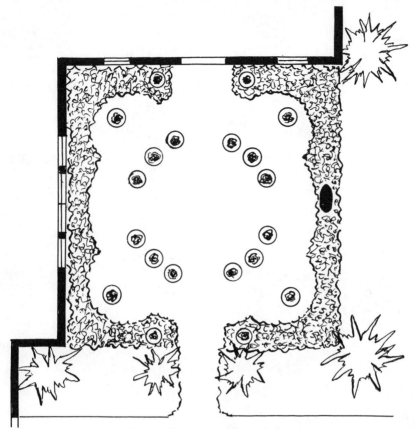

Design for a container garden.

Dooryard gardens are ideal places for container gardening. You can control the rampant spreading of many herbs, such as Mint or Marjoram, by planting them in tubs or tiles. Dwarf fruit trees do well in large tubs, and tree Roses or tree Lilacs make delightful specimens. Containers in wood, pottery, clay, metal, and plastic come in all shapes and sizes. Then there are pieces of driftwood or rocks with hollows, old washtubs or coal scuttles and paint buckets, things to harmonize with any design.

Some people prefer to concentrate on one type of plant, perhaps herbs for gourmet cooking. If Roses are your hobby, make it a Rose garden. In mild climates where soil is acid, Heathers and Heaths make a practically carefree garden. Rabbits seem to be their worst pest. The Heaths (Erica) bloom in winter with small rose, lavender,

A modern design for a dooryard herb garden. *Eloise Ray, L.A.; Molly Adams photo*

or white bells, while Heather (Calluna) starts blooming in June and several varieties will prolong the show of white, pink, and crimson flowers until November. All are evergreen and spreading, although some have golden or reddish leaves in winter.

An all-green dooryard garden can be restful yet full of interest. There is nothing monotonous in the combination of silver-gray-green plants such as Lavender Cotton (*Santolina chamaecyparissus*) with its emerald twin *Santolina viridis*. Lavender (*Lavendula vera*) and the Artemisias are also gray-green and Vinca Minor is a glossy green contrast.

A vegetable garden at the side of the house
can be attractive as well as practical.

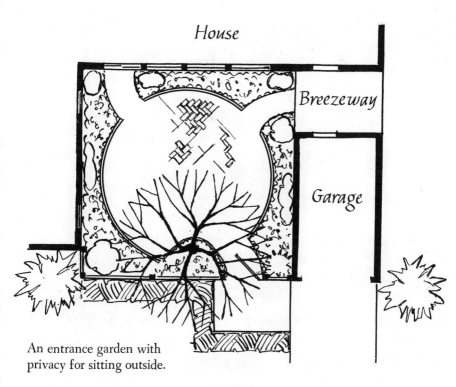

House

Breezeway

Garage

An entrance garden with
privacy for sitting outside.

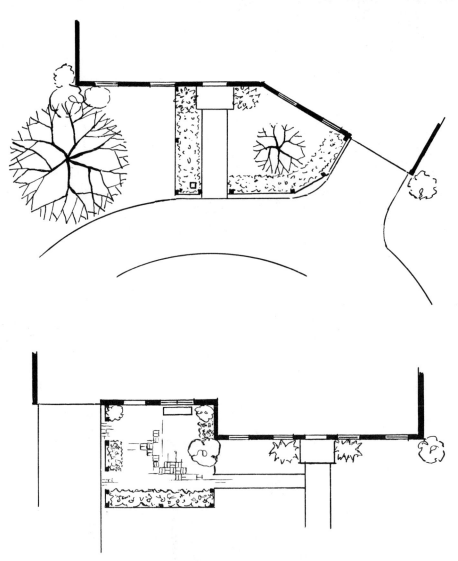

Fences tie dooryard gardens to the house.

Blue-green cushions of Dianthus are a foil for the yellow greens of *Sedum acre* or Moneywort (Lysimachia). There is a handsome bronze-leaved Ajuga to grow with the green or variegated kinds. Dark Opal Basil kept clipped is a dramatic red contrast to woolly gray Lamb's Ears (*Stachys lanata*). Yew grown in the shade is a dark, almost black green which would be interesting with the sunny light green of Boxwood.

There is also a difference in the leaf surfaces to make variety. Some, like Thyme or Artemisia, are dull; Myrtle Ivy and Euonymus are glossy. The texture of the leaves, whether they are coarse or fine, adds interest also. Plantain Lilies (*Hosta*) and Lily of the Valley have large leaves, while Evergreen Candytuft (*Iberis sempervirens*) has fine leaves.

Walks and edgings also play their part in making the design distinctive. You can choose brick in plain, basket-weave, or herringbone patterns for walks, or make walks of gravel with brick or redwood board edging. Paths of flagstone or steppingstones go well with some houses. Wide free-form gravel areas with flagstones are another variation. Plants thrive along paths made of tanbark, and railroad ties make splendid edges where there is room for such heavy construction. Sea shells make a quaint border for a center bed.

There are many different types of enclosure for the garden also: prim picket fences painted white or left to weather naturally for old-fashioned gardens, the strong horizontal lines of post and rail fences to go with the simple lines of modern houses; or a wrought-iron fence for a touch of elegance. Brick or stone walls make good backgrounds for flowers and so do hedges of Yew or Boxwood.

Low-growing plants under a foot high, or those that can easily be kept low, make good edgings to outline beds or for the ribbon designs of knot gardens. Some good plants are:

GRAY FOLIAGE

Lavender Cotton or Ground Cypress (*Santolina chamaecyparissus*). A shrubby perennial with round yellow flowers in June. It will stand hot dry sunny places and poor soil. Zone 7 (see zonal map on p. 172).

Artemisia Silver Mound (*Artemisia schmidt nana*). A moundlike perennial plant with finely cut silvery foliage. Warm, dry, sunny locations suit it well. It dies down in winter. Zone 3.

Lavender (*Lavendula vera*). A very fragrant perennial with narrow silvery leaves. The spikes of lavender flowers last a long time and can be dried to scent linen. Grow it in a sunny place in chalky light loam. Zone 5.

Thyme (*Thymus vulgaris*). A wiry evergreen perennial having narrow aromatic leaves. It will tolerate dry soils and full sun. Zone 5.

Lamb's Ears (*Stachys lanata*). Velvety gray leaves. Cut off flower stalks for a neat appearance. Zone 4.

GREEN FOLIAGE

Germander (*Teucrium chamaedrys*). Many stems from the roots and tiny leaves make this perennial an ideal dwarf hedge plant. It needs good soil and full sun for best results. Zone 6.

Dwarf Boxwood (*Buxus suffruticosa*). Slow-growing shrubs with dense foliage. In the hot sun the leaves have a distinct fragrance. Zone 6.

Korean Boxwood (*Buxus macrophylla*). This is the hardiest Boxwood growing in Zone 5 if protected from strong winds and too much sun.

Chives (*Allium schoenoprasum*). Grassy tubular leaves that taste like onion. The rose-purple flowers are very decorative. It dies down in winter. Zone 3.

Candytuft (*Iberis sempervirens*). Decorative dark green foliage covered with white blossoms at the time the Tulips bloom. It is perennial and evergreen. Zone 3.

Violets (*Viola in var.*). Most thrive in poor soil in shady places. The Bird's-foot Violet grows on dry sunny banks. The leaves disappear in winter. Zone 3.

Dwarf Yaupon (*Ilex vomitoria nana*). Zone 7. Dwarf Japanese Holly (*Ilex crenata helleri*), Zone 6. Two slow-growing Hollies with small glossy leaves.

Lily Turf (*Liriope muscari* or *L. spicata*). In warm climates they have evergreen leaves with spikes of lavender flowers. They do well in sun or part shade.

Pachistima (*Pachistima canbyi*). This little evergreen likes acid soil. The leaves are small and dark green or bronze. Give it partial shade. Zone 5.

Dwarf Cranberrybush (*Viburnum opulus nanum*). Small neat green leaves. Does well in wet heavy clay soil. Zone 3.

Green Santolina (*Santolina viridis*). A feathery emerald green, and a beautiful contrast to the gray variety. Zone 7.

ANNUAL EDGINGS

Parsley, dwarf Marigold, dwarf Periwinkle, Dark Opal Basil if kept clipped.

SIX

Town Houses, Condominiums, and Sky Parks

Although the owner of a town house or condominium cannot do much about landscaping other than dressing up a patio, court, or deck, there is much we can all learn from these building complexes because they are a forward step in land preservation and environmental concern. They have a new freedom of design for a contemporary way of living without conforming to a present style. Architecture and nature blend for better living on less land.

In colonial times people built homes in cities in rows along streets with gardens behind the houses, not because they wanted to save land, which was abundant, but because that was the way town houses were built in Europe. It was convenient, neighborly, and gave a sense of protection. The old town houses in Alexandria, Virginia, are a fine example.

Now we are going back to town houses and condominiums planned in new ways and for new reasons. Building houses in clusters means four, six, or eight to an acre with common walls between, easier maintenance, and lower building costs. Good land planning means that the land saved by putting the houses close together can be turned into large open spaces for the enjoyment of all. Instead of leveling off hills, filling ravines and ponds for house lots, the unusable parts are preserved for natural features, visual interest, and privacy for the area. Each house in the cluster has the maximum visual interest and privacy on a minimum of land.

From the street town houses look co-ordinated, but each is in-

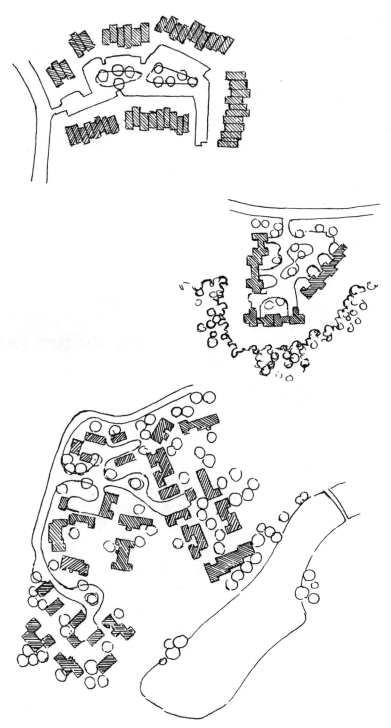

Examples of cluster housing.

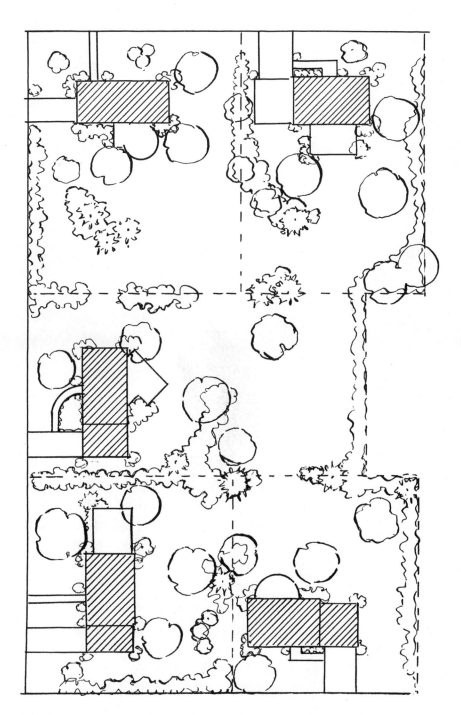

Neighbors in a suburb co-ordinate their landscaping, making a parklike setting with privacy for each and nice vistas. One man can mow the whole area.

Town houses in Marblehead, Mass., reflect the architectural heritage of the town. The planting in front copies the traditional dooryard herb garden. It will always look well and be easy to maintain. *Author*

dividual and inviting. The design may be different for each but the total look is unified in one architectural style, usually keyed to the part of the country in which it is built. Staggered setbacks make room for private entrances and balconies in front, and patios or decks in back. Many have interior garden courts or atriums to let light and a garden view into inside rooms. Each cluster of houses is oriented toward a view of a park, water, or a golf course.

Some condominiums are secluded by eight-foot-high berms heavily planted with trees and shrubs to keep out noise. Curved streets and cul-de-sacs slow traffic, and islands with shady trees and plantings relieve large areas of paving. Although each cluster has an auto arrival space, cars are kept off the landscape as much as possible. Paths and walkways with footbridges enable residents to enjoy the surrounding areas.

Inner courtyards and balconies give the owners of condominiums personal garden space.

Trees shade and camouflage the necessary garages. Planting around each unit varies. Notice the mound and picturesque tree toward the left. *Brown and Kauffmann, Inc.*

A cluster of houses follows the contours of the land down toward a pond. The plans of the houses and the changes in grade give each house a private patio with a view of the pond. *Paparazzo Heritage Corporation*

A rolling countryside and native trees separate clusters of houses. While the whole setting has a unified look, the varying roof pitches and design details individualize the houses. *Paparazzo Heritage Corporation*

Where there is no view outside, the view is oriented to the center of the cluster with a visual focus. Builders transform sites to make charming scenes. Flat sites are changed into hillsides, winding paths open unexpectedly into delightful courtyard gardens with fountains, rose gardens, and pergolas. There are streams with bridges and waterfalls to delight the eye and ear. Rock gardens, arbors, and large trees give the settings a rural look.

In some large condominiums houses are clustered around courtyards in groups of four to six units. The clusters follow the natural contours of the land so that any changes in the natural landscape are reduced to a minimum. Trees and hills make natural separations for the clusters. Each house is planned and turned for maximum privacy. The builders pay special attention to building materials that blend with the environment and unusual architectural details.

A condominium in part of a larger planned community. Live Oaks, Palmettoes, and Pine needles on the ground offer a relaxing environment for retirement, golf, or boating. *Ship Yard Plantation, Hilton Head Island, S.C.*

Many apartment complexes and condominiums achieve variety in atmosphere by stressing both design and activity. Apartments planned for families with small children feature play areas in the parklike center, and balconies with sturdy safe railings. A special school for small children is an additional drawing point.

Some houses are clustered around a yacht basin or a golf course. Riding and winter sports have their devotees. Then there are health spas and retirement villages, sometimes several different condominiums in one large development.

All planting anywhere near a plane must be low enough to go under the wings. Low hedges, ground cover, and flowers, with vines against the house, are ideal. *Sierra Sky Park*

Flying is an activity—you could call it a life style—that calls for a special type of community planning and landscaping. There are several sky parks on the West Coast catering to businessmen who use planes in their daily lives. Some families have two or three planes, and wives, sons, and daughters fly for pleasure. With a plane at the door it is easy to go for a flight any time. In one sky park, lots are adjacent to three sides of an airport with broad streets eighty feet wide (so that two planes can pass) leading to the houses. Planes must restrict taxiing speeds on the streets to ten miles per hour. Some houses have plane ports and some have separate hangars. All planting along the streets has to be less than thirty inches high and the same thing goes for street signs. Mailboxes along the street either pop up to the required height when a triggering device is touched or are counterbalanced so that they tip easily if a plane wing touches them.

House with a plane port.

Another sky park has houses set back along the runway. There is a restriction that no man-made object can be over twenty-four inches high within fifty feet of the runway. Most of the homes in that development have grass out to the runway. The grass is an especially tough variety to take the wear and tear of planes running over it. Landscaping is at a minimum. The developer of one sky park has his house on top of a hangar for three planes.

It is a step from condominiums to planned communities made up of four or five villages, each with residential, recreational, commercial, and industrial areas. The importance of these communities lies in their over-all planning, which takes the environment into consideration. One fifth of the total area is designated for open space, woods, lakes, and recreation. The open spaces blend into all areas, separating clusters of houses and business areas so that every one has an intimate relationship with the land.

They are worth studying as a guide to what you can do on your own property in a more personal way. Make use of all vistas to enlarge your own view. If there is no view or center of interest, make one in an interior court. Above all treat your piece of environment with respect.

SEVEN

Mobile or Modular Homes

A mobile home is a factory-built, completely equipped house supplied with wheels so that it can be towed to its site. It is the quickest and most economical way to get a home. A modular home is trucked to the site in sections and set up according to a variety of floor plans. This takes about two days.

The word "mobile" still gives many people the illusion that these homes are only temporarily on the site, and they are slow to realize the opportunities for making them distinctive with landscaping and accessories. It is a challange and it is fun to make the most of the limited space usually allotted to a mobile home.

The first problem is to make your mobile home look permanently grounded. Metal skirts, masonry walls, and wood siding do a good job of hiding the wheels and utilities and visually relating the home to the ground. They also keep it warmer in winter. Catalogs are helpful with pictures of awnings, steps, railings, and decks, combined with carports, breezeways, and fenced service areas to stretch the living area and make a pleasing transition between the building and its site. Or you can plan your own with rustic wood beams over a wood deck, adding colorful flowers in large clay pots and redwood furniture. You could have white columns in front and a Rose bed with an evergreen hedge, or lacy wrought-iron work and urns of flowers. Where the mobile home is on a large lot the setting in front can follow the designs of larger homes.

A planter full of flowers helps this mobile home to fit its site. *Author*

A mobile home can expand with carport, deck, porch, and storage shed.

The hitch is a fine place to hold a box of Geraniums. *Taloumis*

A wall of concrete blocks widens the base of this mobile home and helps screen the patio. The horizontal metal bar across the top of the window joining the patio and entrance roof ties the combination together at the top. *Vindale Corporation*

Planters make the narrow end of a mobile home look wider. A larger one accents the front door.

Adding a carport is one way of expanding a mobile home. Trees will soon break the line of the flat roof and shade the windows. *Vindale Corporation*

Vines and plants in containers make almost instant landscaping, especially if you start off with an annual vine such as a Morning Glory while a perennial vine gets a good start. Vines take up the least ground space and cover the greatest area of any plant. They quickly soften severe lines. Plant a tree as soon as possible if there are none. Trees are valuable for a feeling of permanence as well as cooling shade in summer.

Planters around part of the foundation are a good-looking way of broadening the base of the foundation. Since the narrow end of a mobile home often faces the street, planters improve the proportions. Make them of cement blocks, brick or stone walls, railroad ties, or redwood sheathing, whatever blends with the building and the scenery. Be sure all footings of walls go below the frost line. One larger planter by the doorway with a handsome specimen plant would be an impressive accent. Combine some evergreens for winter interest with annual flowers for summer color. Add a mulch of wood chips, gravel, cottonseed hulls, or whatever is available locally, and the planters will stay moister and more weed-free.

Curving walks and beds enlarge a small space.

Putting the patio on the other side of the entrance steps divides the space nicely.

Imaginative free-form borders of shrubs and flowers are also a good way of broadening the base and making a mobile home fit its site. Curving outlines make small spaces seem larger than they are. Fill the beds with dwarf or compact varieties of shrubs and evergreens. Put in a ground cover and a small flowering tree for an accent and height. The height of trees helps to break the flat line

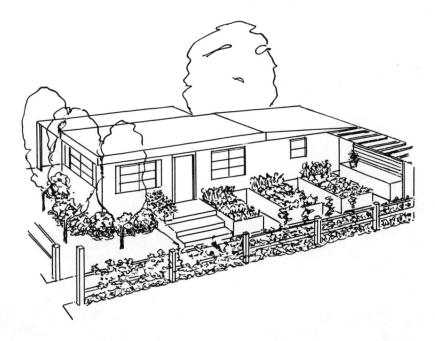

A vest-pocket farm complete with potting shed and tool lockers.

of the roof. A square or rectangular design of beds following the lines of the home always looks orderly and restful.

Where stones are plentiful edge borders with them, and fill in the bed with wood chips that have a coarse texture or gravel. A few pieces of large rock, either natural or Featherlite, or a piece of driftwood with a few green plants tucked in at the base would complete a very decorative picture and one with no care.

If you add a deck, you can walk out of your door at floor level and then make an easy descent with wide shallow steps to a paved area below. A fence surrounding a flagstone- or brick-paved area under a tree would be a pleasant addition to a mobile home. Put a few spring bulbs around the base of the tree and plant shade-tolerant Impatiens, Coleus, or Begonias for summer color.

In a small space too many kinds of plants are distracting. Keep it simple. Choose your favorite plants, relying on evergreens, broad-leaved or needle-leaved, for permanent interest. Concentrate on a hobby garden. Collect the many varieties of Sedums with their suc-

A hanging basket enlivens the doorway. *Taloumis*

culent leaves and long-lasting blooms. Cactus plants are picturesque and easy to care for. Roses, both bushes and vines, are always lovely. Day Lilies now come in many beautiful shades covering a long blooming period during the summer with very little care.

A row of raised beds makes a good growing place for vegetables. Back it with a hedge of Red Currants, Blueberries, or Bush Cherries. A Grapevine on your trellis and a fruit tree will make the whole planting edible.

Prefabricated A-frame houses are quick to build. Many like them for vacation homes. Trees with round or horizontal lines look well against the steep roof pitch.

Container gardening is another hobby that fits in with mobile-home living, especially in mild or warm climates where the pots and plants can stay out all year. There are so many charming containers in many styles to choose from, as well as window boxes and hanging baskets. Bonsai and topiary work are both fun to do if there is not too much other garden work on hand.

Modular houses are built in units that can be arranged on the ground to suit your own floor plan. Although they are standardized, the houses can be large or small, depending on the number of units. Plan the placement so that you have sheltered corners for decks or patios, or an entrance court. It is easy to make these buildings relate to their surroundings when you can allow for trees in the way or changes in grade. If you plan an interior court, keep the planting simple with green underfoot to contrast with floors and paving. A tree for shade and some pots of flowers around a figure or pool would make an interesting view for the windows that open into the court.

There are several different roof elevations on modular homes. The door and window placement is also changeable as is the siding texture. The style is informal, so the planting should reflect that, and follow the basic principles of design.

Some excavating at the front provides an attractive forecourt. Vines coming around the corner and an evergreen in a planter decorate the front of the house.

Instead of terracing in stair-step fashion, contour the slope with mounds that counterbalance the straight lines of the slope. *Oliphant and Kersey, Inc., L.A., Southern Living; Bob Lancaster photo*

EIGHT

Good Grading Is an Asset

Almost every site has some sort of building problem. One as flat as a billiard table may be easy to build on, but it is monotonous and has no drainage. Sloping ground, even that steep enough to cause an architect to tear his hair, can add much beauty and interest to the setting of a house. However, if proper grading is not planned at the start, steep driveways or entrance steps, leaking basements, washed-out plantings, and soggy areas in lawns can be ceaselessly frustrating.

Too often builders set houses on property with no regard for the slope of the land. Then the owner has to do expensive corrective landscaping to fit the house to the site. Other builders and sub-dividers level off property in the interest of easier construction, removing every tree along with the topsoil. Don't let bulldozers level off your lot until you see what can be done to adjust the house to the site. Would that hump give you privacy from the street or camouflage the house next door? Can you make a terrace out of the surplus dirt from the excavation? Bring out the best in the land. Make the house nestle into the curve of a hill, or take advantage of a high spot for a view.

It is important to leave the grades around trees at their existing levels. If you must raise or lower the grade around a tree be very careful. The feeder roots of most trees are six to twelve inches below the surface of the ground. Adding topsoil around a tree cuts off the air supply that the roots need. To fill around a tree success-

Looking out from the house onto the rolling contours. *Southern Living; Bob Lancaster photo*

fully, make a well faced with a dry wall—that is, a wall made without mortar—about a minimum of three to six feet out from the trunk and with the top level with the proposed grade. On the outside of the wall lay a layer of coarse gravel as wide as the outer circumference of the tree branches and about one third the height of the wall. Then fill in with topsoil to the new level. Three quarters of the way out from the trunk of the tree to the outer edge of the branches, put in some six- to eight-inch drain tiles at intervals in a circle around the tree. The tiles should stand on end so that water will run down to the roots of the tree.

If you must cut down the grade around a tree, cut a circle as far out as possible and build a dry wall around it. Any large tree is worth saving. The healthier the tree, the better it will adapt to changing levels.

It is easier and less expensive to plan grading first and do the rough grading at the time the foundation is being dug. In that way you can try to balance the amount of dirt dug out and that to be used for filling in low spots, so that you do not have to buy dirt later on. This also gives the soil a chance to settle, making a more stable foundation for any construction work such as patios, walks, or drives. Dirt needs to settle at least six months before you build on it. Save the topsoil in a pile for finished grading and lawns.

The first consideration in laying out a site is to be sure all water drains away from the house. That is simple if the house is on a rise of ground. If the land slopes toward the house, make a depression lower than the foundation line eight to ten feet out from the house and slope it to one side to carry off water. A slope of one quarter of an inch to a foot will drain. If there is no place for the water to go and the soil absorbs water, make a dry well. A dry well is an underground catch basin or basically a four-by-six hole lined with rock or concrete blocks and filled with large rocks or left empty. Put two layers of pressure-treated one-by-eight boards at right angles to each other over the top. Add roofing felt and a foot of dirt. Before building a dry well find out from the city water department about the level of the water table. If it is less than

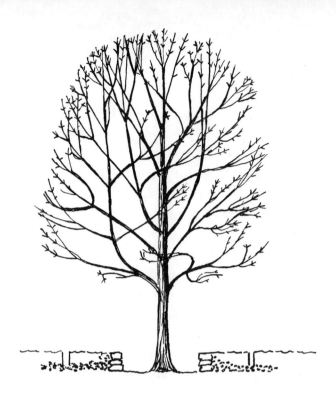

Filling or cutting around a tree.

Grading for land sloping down toward a house.

several feet below the basement floor level, the well would fill with water and be no use. In very flat country where the soil is heavy clay, lay drain tiles a foot or two under the surface and drain them into a storm sewer if one is nearby. This will also take care of water from the gutters. Be careful not to leave any depressions in the lawn where water will stand.

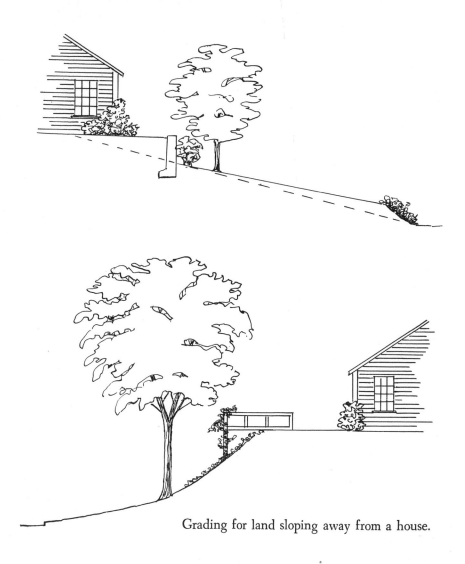

Grading for land sloping away from a house.

When the land slopes away from the house, make a level area or terrace next to the house to give the building a look of stability. A wall or hedge along the edge of the terrace emphasizes the horizontal lines in contrast to the vertical lines of the house. For contemporary houses, decks can be a help in creating the necessary horizontal lines. The warm tones of wood have a natural appearance that blends with house and landscape. Decks practically eliminate the need for foundation planting. You can design decks to fit any

On sloping ground a deck gives a feeling of stability to a house. It does away with the need for planting except at the lower corner. *Author*

area, even letting trees grow up through them. Railings, benches, and steps all add to the decorative design.

Never divide any slope in half. The level part in front of the house should take up only a quarter or third of the space. A very steep slope can have several terraces with retaining walls or banks covered with ground cover in between levels.

A house well below the grade of the street needs to take advantage of its site especially by making efficient use of the various levels to plan for the easiest driveway and garage entrance with a flat area in which to turn the car. Keep the grades in proper relation to the floor levels of the house so that you can walk out easily on various floor levels.

A low retaining wall curves informally among the trees.

It is not always desirable to have a retaining wall for each change in grade.

Two walls hold up a bank with an easily accessible place for a flower garden in between. *Cartie*

A formal approach for a house below the level of the street; having the walk turn at right angles twice makes the descent seem more gradual. *Arkansas Gazette; Gene Prescott photo*

Relate the floors inside the house to the levels outside.

Many times land slopes across the front of the house from one side to another. Split-level houses fit well into such a terrain, but not everyone wants a split-level house, so some way must be found to make the slope look pleasing against the house and keep the plantings from looking as though they were sliding downhill. Planters are one solution for camouflaging changes in grade. Either next to the house or along the edge of a patio or terrace, they keep the planting in a horizontal line with the house. Variations in the heights of plants also help. Tall shrubs or small flowering trees, especially those with multiple trunks, minimize the drop at the low end of the house. Vines on horizontal trellises will carry a line of green across the face of the house. They will also cover a high foundation and make it harmonize with the ground.

A split-level house takes advantage of a slope. Carry the planting of ground cover on the slope up onto the level lawn in front of the house to tie the plan together.

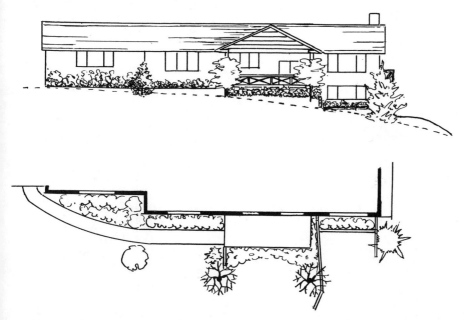

Plan and front elevation of a house with grading following the horizontal lines of the house. Railroad-tie walls come out into the lawn to meet the existing grades.

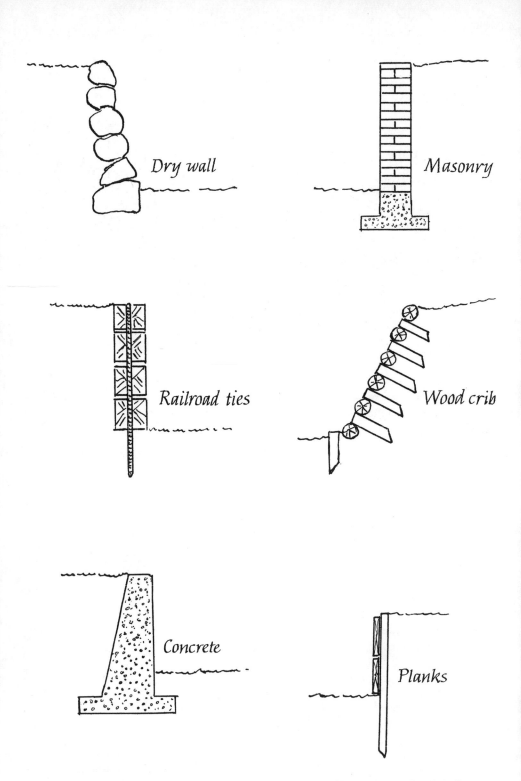

Stair-step fences, walls, and hedges on a slope. Increase the height of plants as the line of the foundation drops, so that the tops are horizontal.

A berm between the street and drive will soon provide privacy and noise control when the plants grow. There is another mound in front of the window which hides the drive. *William Aplin*

Sometimes in the interests of privacy and noise control you might want to build an artificial mound to screen the house from the street or at the back to shield a patio. This can be a gentle slope starting from a level area near the house, rising to a point three quarters of the way across the lawn, then falling down in a steeper grade with a bank or retaining wall at the street. Plant the mound thickly with trees and shrubs. The mound makes a pleasant view from the house as well as effectively muffling the noise from the street.

135

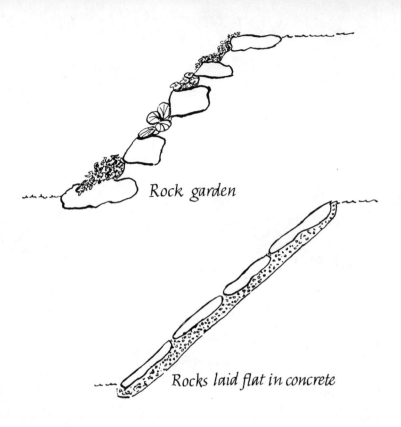

Rock garden

Rocks laid flat in concrete

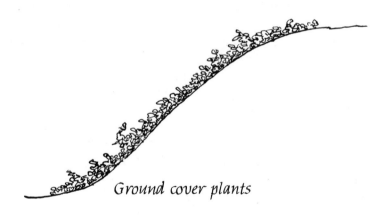

Ground cover plants

Three ways to keep a bank from eroding.

A wall takes up much less room than a bank. *Author*

For a small area a rock garden ten feet wide and five feet high with shrubs on top does the same thing. It can be curved in an informal way, and it is just as pretty on either side.

Any slope of more than one foot rise to two feet of run is hard to maintain. Plan to cover it with a ground cover or low shrubs, or break it with a wall. You can make walls of rock laid dry without mortar, or masonry walls of stone or brick. All walls need a footing to go below the frost line, and drainage holes at the base every eight to ten feet. Railroad ties or log cribbing make more informal walls.

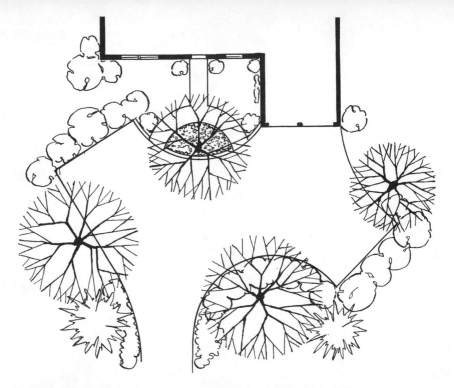

Integrate the parking area and turnaround with the design.

Here an unpaved driveway blends so well with the landscape that it does not seem to take up much room. *Port Royal Plantation, Hilton Head Island, S.C.*

NINE

Driveways, Parking Areas, Walks, and Steps

Driveways and Parking Areas

Most visitors get their first impression of your home as they drive up to your front door. The impression will be a pleasant one if, in addition to good planting, the entrance curves easily into the drive and there is ample room to park. Next to the lawn, the driveway takes up the largest amount of space in front of the house. Adding parking room makes it even larger, but you can make it attractive as well as practical by incorporating it into the total design.

Many cities pave driveway entrances along city streets according to their specifications, so the entrance curve is fixed. A short turn means that as you approach your driveway on the right you will have to swing into the opposite lane of traffic to turn in easily. The same thing happens when you come out of the drive and turn right. This can be dangerous. If you can plan your own entrance, make the curve of the turning radius an eighteen-foot minimum. A single drive can be ten feet wide although twelve feet is more ample. For a double drive or one with parking along the side, make it twenty feet wide.

Keep any planting at the entrance low for good visibility, and leave a space between any planting and the paving for getting in and out of the car. A name and number plate that can be read from a car is helpful. It is hard to read house numbers by the front door as you drive down the street.

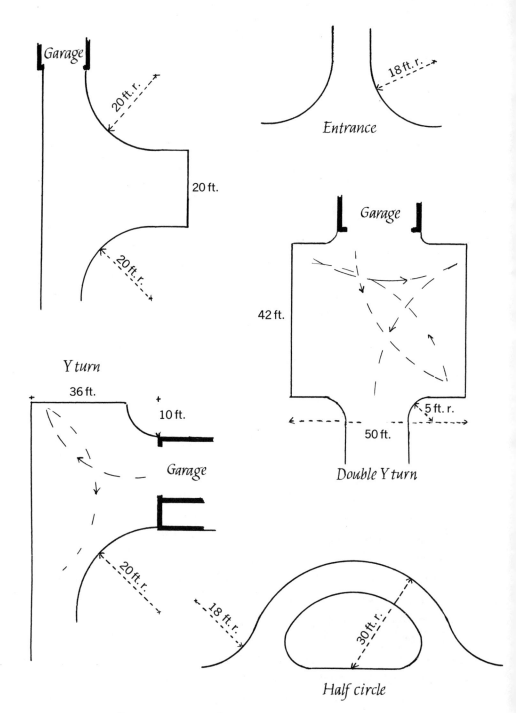

Garage

20 ft. r.

20 ft.

20 ft. r.

Entrance

18 ft. r.

Garage

42 ft.

5 ft. r.

50 ft.

Double Y turn

Y turn

36 ft.

10 ft.

Garage

20 ft. r.

18 ft. r.

30 ft. r.

Half circle

Driveway details showing minimum radii for turns.

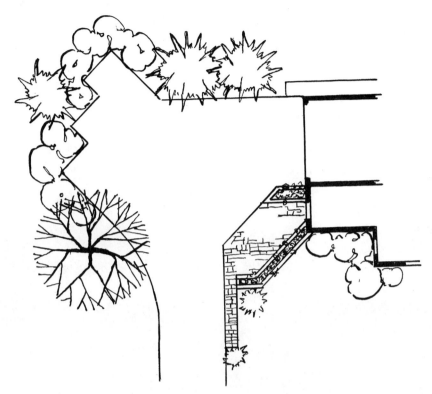

A paved entranceway with a planter is inviting. Place the house at one side of the lot to make room for parking and turnaround.

Many driveways include the entrance walk. Where the walk leaves the drive to go to the front door, make an inviting and generous approach that ties the driveway and house together. Visitors will automatically head in the right direction and not wonder where the front door is. Have adequate access for service and deliveries. Remember that large equipment such as appliances must go in the back or side door, and trash must be removed.

Steep grades cause consternation in slippery weather. Adapt the level of the garage to the grade as much as possible even if that makes it on a different level from the house. Cutting a driveway along the diagonal line of a slope makes an easier grade.

Leave room beside the driveway for loading and unloading cars, and make the entrance steps ample and welcoming. Yew leads the eye up toward the front door. The slope is covered with ground cover (Euonymus) and Juniper. A Flowering Dogwood is a focal point at the right of the doorway. *Genereux*

To get up a steep grade to a garage, curve the driveway diagonally up the front lawn.

Off-street parking has become a necessity rather than a luxury. Even without allowing for guests, there are extra family cars, boats, campers, etc., to be taken care of. Plan for extra parking when you plan the garage and drive, and get as much as possible.

Where city ordinances permit, do not be afraid to use up lawn area in front of the house for parking. On the minimum thirty-foot setback for houses specified in many cities and towns, that means either paving most of the front yard or trying to get parking space on the side. As long as it is not too conspicuous from picture windows and is camouflaged by shrubs it will be attractive. Also what you pave you do not have to mow, and in the quest for easily maintained gardens these days, that is something to think about.

Each parked car will need a minimum of twenty-two by eight feet. Diagonal parking is easy. Make the slots at a sixty-degree angle or forty-five if there is more room to back and turn. If the garage is close to the street it will be necessary to back out into the street to turn. However, if it is at all possible fix it so that you can turn and come out into the traffic front first.

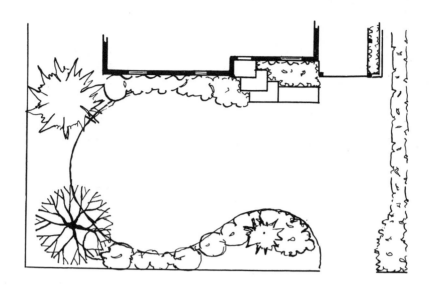

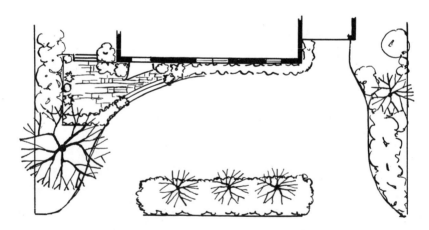

Where city ordinances permit, use the space in front of the house for extra parking. Screen it from the street.

OPPOSITE ABOVE:
Make parking room for an extra car on a small lot.
BELOW:
A Y-turn fits around a front terrace with an easy ramp walk.

144

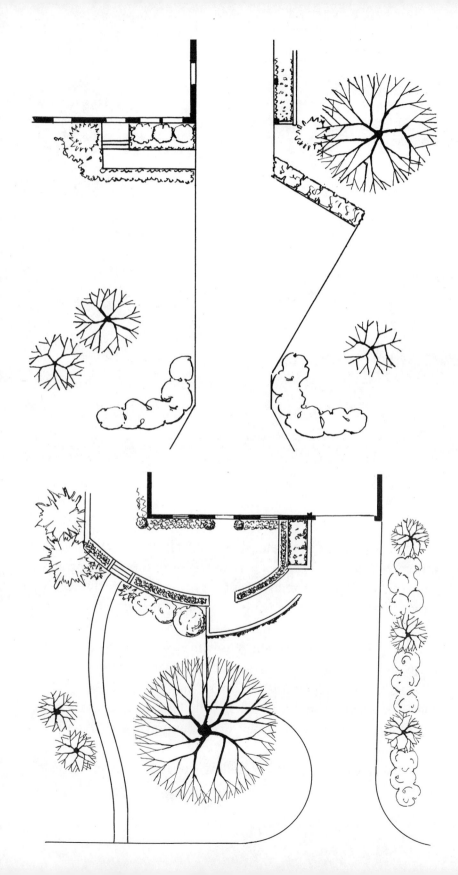

Blacktop (asphalt) covers a large parking area without glare. *Cabot Stains; R. Wenken photo*

Gravel, blacktop, concrete, or paving blocks are all good driveway materials if properly laid. Driveways are a permanent and expensive part of the garden layout. Plan and construct them well. Large areas of concrete paving are glaring to look at. This is especially bad in front of a picture window. You can add texture and cut the glare by brushing concrete with a stiff brush or marking it in swirls with a trowel. Do not try that in cold climates as water collects in the depressions, freezes, and plays havoc with the concrete, causing it to break up. In mild climates exposed aggregate has a pleasing texture and color depending on the sizes and colors of the embedded stones.

You can cut the glare by adding color to concrete. Applying

Break up parking spaces with planting beds. Gravel needs a neat edge. The whole parking area is divided from the lawn by a decorative stone wall. *Taloumis*

powdered pigment to the cement as it is being mixed, or you can paint concrete that has already been laid with paints especially made for concrete. Green and shades of tan are restful to the eye. Large areas of paving reflect heat. Break them up with islands of planting and have trees in the islands for shade. Paving is also monotonous. Divide large spaces into sections with redwood two-by-four headers that can serve as expansion joints or parking lines. You can also use brick or concrete block lines. Make designs in the paving with contrasting textures and colors.

For easy mowing keep the edges of the driveway paving flush with the lawn. Gravel drives need curbs or edges of metal, brick, or concrete to keep them neat.

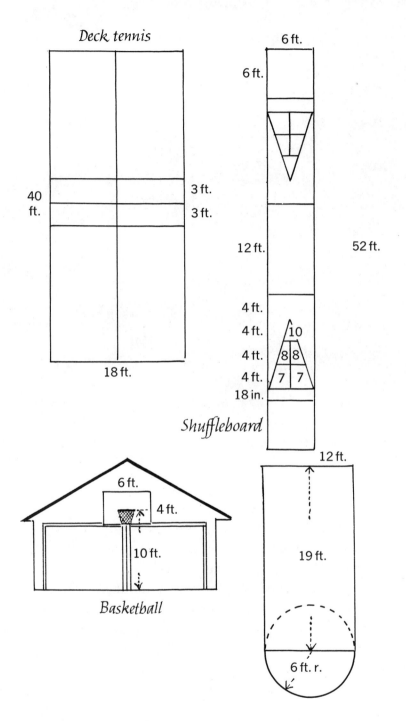

Measurements for games to play on paved drives.

148

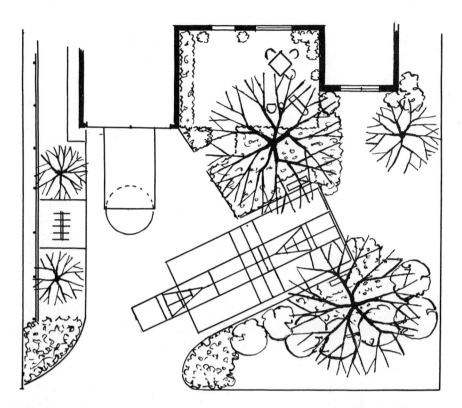

So much paving can lead a double life. It makes a fine play place for children to ride tricycles, bounce a basketball, skip rope, play shuffleboard or deck tennis. Have benches for spectators. It can also double as an extra patio area.

Walks

Walks and steps are also important parts of the landscaping plan in front. For two people to walk side by side, a walk needs to be four feet wide; five would be better. Use a paving material that blends with the house and the effect you wish to achieve. Brick laid in sand or mortar makes a warm inviting walk. Cut stone is dignified, irregular flagstone more casual. Steppingstones in gravel with a border of concrete brick are economical, while wooden rounds or paving blocks fit a rustic atmosphere. Concrete, plain or with exposed aggregate, is durable and carefree. If the lawn is small, make the walk as straight as possible. Combining the walk with the driveway saves cutting the lawn in two.

Any walk is only as good as its foundation, so plan it carefully. Lay out the outline accurately with forms. Use two-by-fours for straight edges with stakes every two or three feet. Exterior grade plywood or Masonite will make curved forms. For brick, stone, or patio blocks, prepare the subgrade five to eight inches below the finished grade. Fill in with a layer of gravel or crushed stone and then two inches of sand, bringing up the level to three inches below the finished grade.

In areas where drainage is good two to three inches of sand, will be enough without the gravel layer. When you order sand, figure out the cubic yards you need and double the order. You will wonder where it is all going but it packs down.

Many women enjoy laying brick paving since the bricks are easy to handle. Four and one half bricks make a square foot. There are several patterns: plain, basket weave, and herringbone. After you put in the sand, tamp it down hard, wet it, fill in and level the grade, tamp and wet it again. Lay the borders first and see that they are level with one another. As you put in the bricks add more sand and pound each brick in tight and solid with a hammer and board. Never hit a brick directly with a hammer. Use a straight piece of two-by-four to put a mason's level on, and check continuously to see that your paving is smooth. Do a small area at a time. A

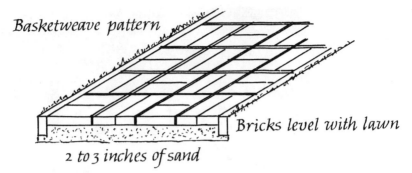

Basketweave pattern

Bricks level with lawn

2 to 3 inches of sand

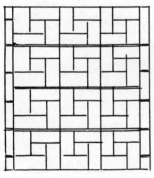

Plain pattern,
can also be horizontal

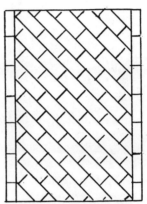

Diagonal pattern

Spanish pattern

Herringbone pattern

Brick walks.

Brick laid in sand for a walk contrasts with stone steps. A railing is especially good in cold climates. *Don Wells*

slope of one quarter of an inch to a foot drains well. When the walk is done, sweep dry sand into the cracks, wet it, and repeat.

Brick or stone laid in mortar requires a three- to four-inch layer of reinforced concrete base on top of a layer of gravel or crushed rock. You can lay the bricks as soon as the concrete can bear your weight. Spread a half-inch mortar bed for several bricks at a time.

Unless you are an expert, it is better to have a contractor pour concrete walks. It is heavy work that has to be done quickly and finished smoothly with special tools. A cement company will be glad to give you advice on doing one in your part of the country, if you feel like undertaking the job.

Steps

Garden steps relate in scale to the outdoor scene and need to have wider treads and shallower risers than interior steps. Treat even the usual materials in interesting ways, making use of textures and edgings for effect. Railroad ties with gravel, brick or asphalt make attractive steps. Large wood rounds and worn flagstones with creeping plants at the edges are other ways of making a feature of your steps.

The steepness and width of the slope will determine the size of the steps. For best results the proper proportion is based on the average length of stride, and that works out to a formula of *twice the riser plus the tread should equal twenty-six inches*. Therefore if you have a riser of six inches the tread will be fourteen inches. A five-inch riser has a tread of sixteen inches, and a four-inch riser a tread of eighteen inches. Spaces between flights of steps should be figured in multiples of strides: fifty-two inches, seventy-eight inches.

To measure the height of a small slope, take two stakes, a line level, and mason's twine. Pound in one stake at the top of the slope. Tie the twine to the stake at ground level and measure out three feet, keeping the twine tight and level as you go down the slope. Pound in another stake and tie the twine very tightly at the same level as the first. Measure the distance to the ground and note it on a chart. Pull up the first stake and repeat the process until you reach the bottom of the slope. Draw the resulting measurements on a chart to scale, so many inches or feet down for each three feet, and you will have a diagram of your slope from which to plan your steps.

Foundations of steps are important. For any masonry make footings to go below frost. Start building steps from the bottom.

Espaliered Pyracantha fills a blank wall with dramatic effect. *Author*

TEN

Distinctive Plant Material

In order to create a beautiful setting for your home you need to know your plant materials and how best to use them. Learn to recognize the design possibilities of trees and shrubs because they are the structural elements you use.

Form

The most important element is form or shape, for it is permanent and very strong, leading the eyes where you want them to look. When you plan the planting around your house think first of the shape of plant you need in each place. It helps to make a diagrammatic sketch of the walls and try out various forms against them. Plants come naturally in every shape but square, it seems. What you don't find in the lists at the end of this section, you can make by training and pruning.

Dramatic forms make accents where you want to call attention to a front entrance or relieve the monotony of a large blank wall. Perfectly round balls are dramatic, and tall narrow spires add emphasis. Irregular or picturesque forms call attention to themselves, and man-made shapes espaliered or trained are striking. The darker the color and the denser the foliage, the more dramatic the form will be.

Billowy outlines and overarching forms help to tie down a house. Multiple trunks break up and confuse the strong vertical lines at

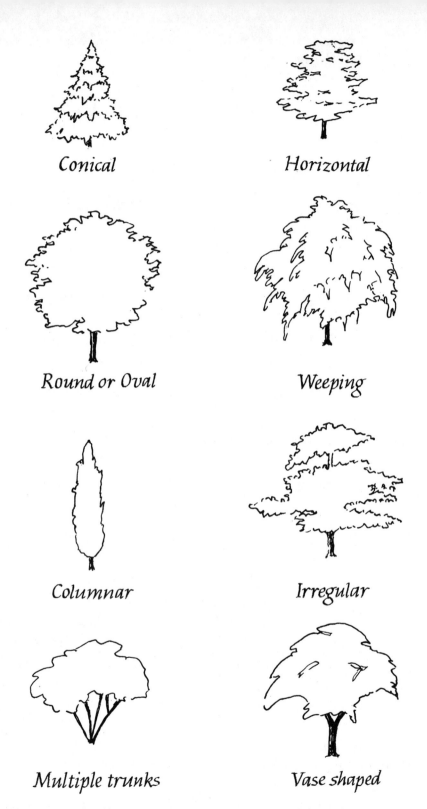

Conical

Horizontal

Round or Oval

Weeping

Columnar

Irregular

Multiple trunks

Vase shaped

Forms of trees. Shrubs are similar with the addition of prostrate or creeping forms.

Rounded forms and small trees with multiple trunks soften and tie down the corners of a house.

Multiple trunks of a tree shown off against a chimney. *Edward D. Stone and Associates*

the corners of buildings. They seem to reduce the height. Wide-spreading shrubs broaden an area. To lift the eye toward a view or away from some sight, use a strong uplifting line. Weeping lines carry the line of sight down and there should always be something at the base of a Weeping Willow, or better yet a Weeping Cherry, which does not have such a destructive root system.

Some deciduous trees have definite branch patterns in winter that make dramatic forms. Flowering Dogwood has branches that grow in layers so that it makes a beautiful horizontal pattern against a wall. Use it for a broadening effect in a narrow space. Staghorn Sumac is interesting all year, but really striking when the leaves are gone and you can see the thick picturesque branches. Regel's Privet has a spreading, rather oriental look in winter quite different from its summer aspect. The Winged Euonymus grown for its glorious red fall coloring has a very distinctive cinnamon-colored corky bark on its arching branches.

Texture

The next design element to consider is texture, whether the leaves are coarse or fine. The sizes of leaves range all the way from the giant Palm fronds and the huge leaves of Evergreen Magnolia to the tiny round leaves of Dwarf Japaneses Holly var. *Helleri*. You can see how much more emphasis a plant with large leaves would give to a scene. If it is evergreen it would be as dramatic as a strong form in calling attention to a special spot.

Use bold patterns with restraint. If large texture predominates it will make the space seem smaller and the design too busy. If you need more plants add larger quantities of smaller-textured plants, graduating the texture from large to medium and then small so that there will not be a sudden contrast. Any type of foliage becomes monotonous if there is no variety.

The glossy shine of broad-leaved evergreens makes the texture stand out more than the dull matte surface of deciduous leaves. The shapes of deciduous leaves and the habits of growth add more interest.

There are other textures in the landscape as well: the wood, brick, or stone walls of the house, gravel, stone, and concrete on the ground. Think of these also as you decide which plants to use. Pictures in books and catalogs as well as plants in nurseries will help you choose.

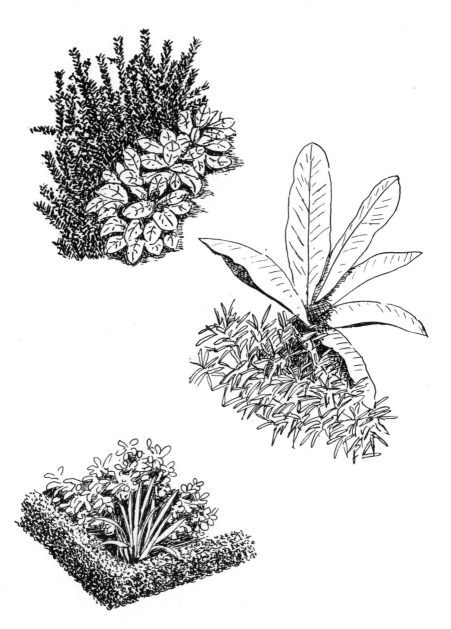

Differences in textures of leaves.

The coarse texture of Fatshedera on a garden gate contrasts with the finer textures of the shrubs below. *Roche photography*

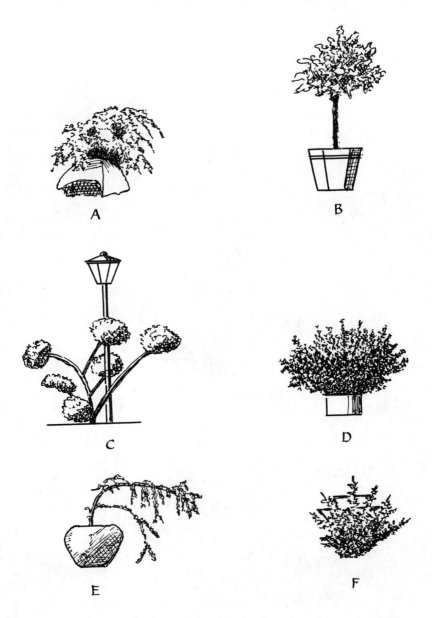

Various ways of using shrubs. A. Weeping shrub with rocks. B. Standard tree form in a tub. C. Poodle cut for decoration. D. Spreading shape of Yew accentuated by snug container. E. Graceful lines in a round bowl. F. Creeping Juniper trained upright.

Scale

The size of plants in relation to the house and area to be planted can make or break a plan. Learn the ultimate height and size of all plants before you plant them. That cute little evergreen in its nursery container may grow into a forest giant, and the Pyracantha so neatly trained to a stake grows so fast where the climate suits it that it needs lots of room or ruthless pruning every year. Clipping an evergreen that is meant to be a tree year after year weakens it, and as the trunk grows larger it becomes very unattractive. So much trimming also ruins the natural habit of growth. It is better to start with an evergreen that will not grow tall or is very slow-growing. There are dwarf conifers and slow-growing Yews that stand shearing well. If you have a large Pine or Spruce that is taking up too much room or covering a window and you want to keep it, cut off the lower branches. The trunk and top will not take up so much room. In the forest nature eventually does the same thing.

The size of plants will set the scale for your garden. A large tree will dominate the scene and make the house and garden seem smaller. A small house looks cozy under a large tree. A tall massive building needs large trees around it to look right. Several small trees would make a small house look larger, anything too small would look ridiculous.

If you have large trees around your house, too many other large shrubs would be monotonous. As in texture, graduate the scale of the plants. Remember that the lawn area has the finest texture and scale, and large areas of lawn will balance large-scale plants. The shadows of trees are beautiful on a carpet of green grass.

Planting mature trees or shrubs is expensive and not always easy. If you are impatient for results, plant what nurserymen call specimen shrubs of a good size at the most important points, perhaps at the front door, and wait awhile longer for the rest. You can add extra shrubs to fill in, planning to remove them later to other places reserved on the plan as others mature.

Color

Most people think of color first in relation to plants. They buy a yellow Forsythia, a pink Azalea, or a purple Lilac. Although color is the most showy quality of plants, it lasts a very short time during the year. Some plants have several seasons of color: flowers in spring, leaves in fall, and berries in winter. Others, such as Purple Plum and Red Barberry, have dark red leaves all summer.

Short as the season is, the wrong color can clash with other colors, especially those inside the house. If you are fond of orange and yellow in your interior decorating do not plant a magenta Redbud or Rhododendron just outside the window. Choose colors that harmonize or contrast well with the siding and trim of the house as well as the colors inside. Use white or pale colors against dark walls and brighter colors against white. Put other colors you like near a green background. There are times when the shadow lines of the tree in winter or the beauty of the foliage, which lasts for months, will offset the choice of a poor color, which lasts only a week or two. Think of the form and texture first, then the color.

Unity

In plants you would consider unity in an ecological sense. Do your plants look as though they belonged in the same environment? Can you imagine, for instance, a White Pine and a Cactus together? Plants as growing things are naturally related by their environment: shade-loving woody plants, desert-tolerant species, those that will stand bright sun, and plants that need wet roots.

Deciduous shrubs and trees growing in forests have lighter green leaves than those growing in bright sunlight. In marshes colors are yellow green, while desert plants are grayish with very bright, often magenta flowers. If you use plants in groupings that live well together, not only will your design be satisfactory, but the plants will grow better because they all like the same conditions. To leave part of the property in a wild state make a demarcation with plants in a

The Pine hedge, Ivy ground cover, flagstone entrance step, and Cedar gate all form a unified composition. *Roche photography*

border or low hedge, or build a low wall between the cultivated and wild parts.

With so many people moving from one part of the country to another each year, learning what will do well in a new climate is a problem. Native plants always do well. It may be hard to give up Lilacs, but the reward may be Crape Myrtle or Gardenias. Don't fight it, join it. There are beautiful plants and ways of gardening for every climate, dry, shady, arctic, or seashore. Find out from the nearest nurseryman what the best plants are, and notice what is thriving in neighborhood gardens.

Each side of your house will have a microclimate that is different. There will be sunny, shady, windy, or sheltered sides, and you should choose plants that will tolerate each condition. If a plant is not reliably hardy put it on the east or north side of the house where it will stay dormant until the weather is warm. In parts of the country where the weather in winter swings from warm to cold and then warm again almost overnight, this is especially important.

Deciduous shrubs predominate in the North where there is deep snow. Either the shrubs are buried in deep snow or the snow and ice mantles the branches in a layer of beauty. The leaves of broad-leaved evergreens under such conditions look abused. You can almost tell the temperature by the amount of curl in the Rhododendron leaves in cold weather. Many deciduous shrubs also have berries that are colorful in winter as well as providing food for the birds.

Pollution is a new factor that plays no favorites with climates. Where pollution is bad pay attention to the list of pollution-tolerant shrubs and trees at the end of this section. Again, consult your local nurseryman. Pollution shows in spotted, streaked, and bleached foliage, and tan or white lesions on leaf margins or in between veins, or retarded growth. When you see signs of pollution cut down on nitrogen fertilizer, which stimulates growth but increases sensitivity to pollution. Use only moderate fertilization and watering to help the plants survive.

To summarize:
    Begin with a plan.
    Use form for accent,
        texture for interest,
        evergreens, either broad-leaved or needle-leaved, for weight,
        deciduous or flowering shrubs for seasonal interest,
        berried shrubs for winter.
    Consider the size and scale of plants.
    Choose colors in relation to both the inside and outside of the house after thinking of other factors.
    Choose plants that like the same environment.
    Watch out for pollution.

Planting the Front of the House

The first thing in the way of landscaping that a new owner does is to put some shrubs in front of the house. It gives the house a lived-in look as curtains do inside. Unfortunately too many people, in their haste to cover up the bare look, buy the plants most easily accessible, overplant, and plant too close to the foundation. There the plants have no room to develop and do not get enough moisture under the eaves. A few well-chosen shrubs and evergreens will do more for a house than a lot of mediocre small ones all in a row. Even one Euonymus vine and a Pyracantha rightly used would take care of a house.

Concentrate on the entrance first. If you do a good job on that, the rest can wait a bit. After considering the shape you want, an interesting texture and perhaps a color, be sure the plants are good-looking twelve months of the year. They do not always have to be evergreen, but if they are deciduous they should have winter interest. Regel's Privet, Alpine Currant, Red Twig Dogwood, dwarf *Euonymus alatus,* and Inkberry are all good.

Many new varieties of low-growing and dwarf shrubs are appearing at the nurseries and in the catalogs in response to the demand, so it should be easy to find those that will not outgrow their welcome. Good catalogs specify heights so you will have some idea of what you are buying. There will be a list at the end of this section.

Put in only enough planting to make the house look comfortable in its location. Sometimes you may need shrubs to conceal a bad point or to give privacy to an area near the house, but functional parts of the building, even window wells, are not bad-looking. Planting around them would cut out the light and air they are supposed to supply. Chimneys on the outer walls of the house can have a vine or espaliered shrub for decoration, but nothing that will add to the bulk. The idea is not to cover up the foundation but to accent important spots and tie the house down with rounded shrubs, groupings of plants, or small trees with multiple trunks.

167

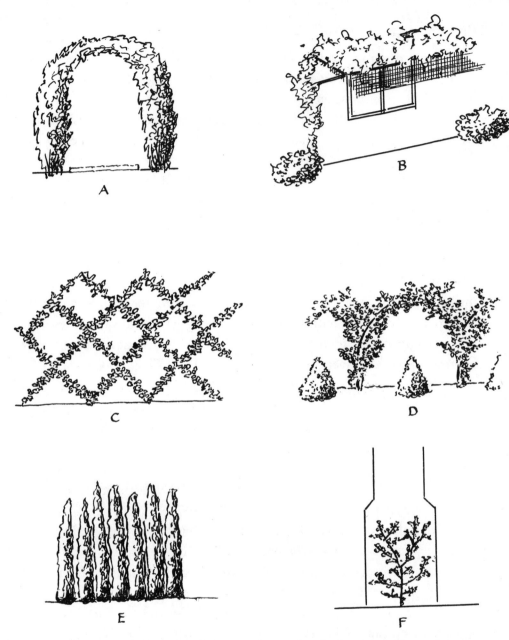

Make use of the natural habits of growth of plants: A. For making an arch. B. Vines as awnings over a window. C. Vines trained on wires against a bare wall. D. Rose vines arch to frame a feature. E. Grow your own fence with tall narrow evergreens. F. Decorate a chimney with a natural espalier.

Vines perform many functions. They make a tracery pattern on bare walls, change the lines of a building, and hide any faults by concealing or correcting proportions. They also soften the texture of hard walls. The foliage helps keep walls cool in summer. If there is no soil for planting at the base of a wall, you can train a vine to come around a corner and add some green to the space. Vines can also be nuisances if you pick the wrong one. Wisteria, which twines, needs a very strong trellis or support to climb on. It will squash a drainpipe flat. Never put Baltic Ivy (*Hedera helix*) on a wood wall; it climbs by clinging and it is impossible to get it off without ruining the paint. In fact it is hard on brick too, and should be controlled so that it does not completely smother the house. Boston Ivy (*Parthenocissus tricuspidata*) and Virginia Creeper (*Parthenocissus quinquefolia*) are easier to control. You can stand on the ground and pull them down, cut them off at the roots, and in a year or two they will be up to the top of the chimney again.

Rose vines need the support of a trellis. Clematis, Fleece Vine, and Honeysuckle have to have something to twine on. Euonymus will climb a short way by fastening itself to a wall, then it needs help with clamps or something to support it. If you have a house that has to be painted periodically, grow vines on trellises that can be taken down or are hinged to lie flat.

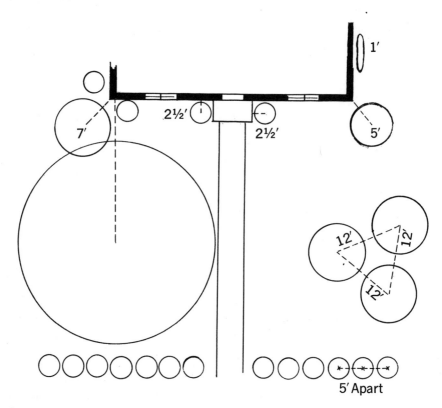

5' Apart

Spacing for planting: 2½ feet out from the walls is a minimum for foundation plants. 5 feet for larger shrubs at the corner. 7 feet for small tree at the corner. 12 feet between small trees in a group. 1 foot for a vine or espalier. 5 feet apart for flowering shrubs in a border. 1 foot apart for trimmed hedges. 24 feet out from the house for an average tree. Tall narrow trees and those with overarching branches can be closer.

Have your planting far enough out from the eaves so that the overhang does not cut off moisture. Two and a half feet out is a good minimum. If the eaves are very wide, have a walk or gravel strip along the side of the house and move the planting out beyond that. You can plant ground cover, a creeping kind like Baltic Ivy, at the outer edge and let it grow back toward the foundation to cover the ground. Cultivate all the area between the wall and the outer edge of the planting and mulch it. Mulching will keep

Use mulch or ground cover from the foundation line out to the edge of the planting. A mowing strip makes trimming easier.

in the moisture, inhibit the weeds, keep dirt from splashing on the walls in a storm, and generally keep it well groomed.

Choose plants for your front planting that harmonize with your house and life style. If you like everything elegant and well groomed, choose plants that are slow-growing and neat in habit. For a more casual, relaxed look and a house of stone or natural wood siding, choose plants that look informal and more picturesque.

Consider the exposure, whether it is a west wall with hot sun, light shade under a tree, or deep shade on the north. Few plants need shade, but some will tolerate it well. There is a plant for every place and every purpose. The variety is abundant, so there is no excuse for monotony, and you can have a setting that suits you.

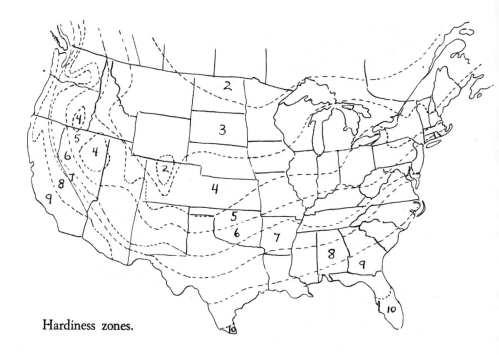

Hardiness zones.

Hardiness

Hardiness zones show the cold tolerance of plants. They do not take into consideration dry conditions, salt air, excessive moisture or heat. The number given after a plant name is the northern limit, and plants will grow well several zones south. In California one can grow almost anything. Plants from cold zones do not grow well in hot climates; in fact deciduous shrubs look dead in winter where everything else is green. Hardiness varies even within zones, so it pays to check locally.

A Classified Listing

I FORM

A. *Horizontal Lines* Zone

		Zone
White Pine	*Pinus strobus*	2
Black Locust	*Robinia pseudoacacia*	2
Cockspur Hawthorn	*Crataegus crus-galli*	3
Flowering Dogwood	*Cornus florida*	5
Doublefile Viburnum	*Viburnum tomentosum* var. *mariesi*	4
Regel's Privet	*Ligustrum obtusifolium* var. *regeleanum*	5
Blue Spruce	*Picea pungens*	3
	Spruce has horizontal branches in a pyramidal form	
Sassafras	*Sassafras albidum*	4

B. *Picturesque Trees with Character*

Blue Gum	*Eucalyptus globulus*	9
Camphor Tree	*Cinnamomum camphora*	8
Corkscrew Willow	*Salix matsudana*	3
Black Locust	*Robinia pseudoacacia*	2
Japanese Black Pine	*Pinus sylvestris*	3
Japanese Snowbell	*Styrax japonica*	6
Monkey Puzzle	*Araucaria imbricata*	8
Monterey Pine	*Pinus radiata*	8
Nikko Fir	*Abies homolepis*	6
Sour Gum	*Nyssa sylvatica*	6
Jacaranda	*Jacaranda acutifolia*	10
Pepper Tree	*Schinus molle*	8
Palms	Palms species	10
Golden Rain	*Koelreuteria paniculata*	5

B2. *Smaller Sizes of Picturesque Trees*

Red Jade Crabapple	*Malus* Red Jade	3
Tea Crabapple	*Malus hupehensis*	3
Dracaena	*Dracaena marginalis*	9
Sea Grape	*Coccolobis uvifera*	10
Tree Wisteria	Wisteria tree form	5
Japanese Maple	*Acer palmatum*	6
Devil's Walking Stick	*Aralia elata*	3
Staghorn Sumac	*Rhus typhina*	3
Screw Pine	*Pandanus utilis*	10
Cactus	Cactus species	8–9

173

C. *Pyramidal*

1 EVERGREEN TREES

Cedar (White) *Thuya occidentalis*	2
Cedar (Red) *Juniperus virginiana*	3
Deodar Cedar *Cedrus deodara*	7
Fir (White) *Abies concolor*	5
Fir (Douglas) *Pseudotsuga taxifolia*	4
Hemlock *Tsuga canadensis*	2–3
Holly (American) *Ilex opaca*	5
Spruce *Picea* species	3
Yew *Taxus cuspidata*	4
Bottle Tree *Sterculia diversifolia* semi-evergreen	7

2 DECIDUOUS

Pin Oak *Quercus palustris*	5
Sweet Gum *Liquidambar styraciflua*	4
Sycamore *Platanus occidentalis*	5
Chanticleer Pear *Pyrus calleryana* Chanticleer	5

D. *Vase-shaped*

1 TREES

American Elm *Ulmus americana*	4
Moraine Locust *Gleditsia triacanthos inermis* var. Moraine	3
Scholar Tree *Sophora japonica*	5
Hackberry *Celtis occidentalis*	4
Silver Maple *Acer saccharinum*	4
Zelkova *Zelkova serrata*	5
Tea Crabapple *Malus hupehensis*	3

2 SHRUBS

Bridal Wreath *Spiraea vanhouttei*	3
Abelia *Abelia grandiflora*	5
Forsythia *Forsythia* species	5

E. *Weeping*

1 TREES

Weeping Beech *Fagus sylvatica pendula*	4
Weeping Birch *Betula pendula*	2
Cutleaf Birch *Betula pendula gracilis*	2
Camperdown Elm *Ulmus glabra camperdownii*	4
Weeping European Hornbeam *Carpinus betulus pendula*	4
Weeping Cherry *Prunus serrulata pendula* and *Prunus subhirtella higan*	4
Weeping Silver Linden *Tilia petiolaris*	4
Weeping Norway Spruce *Picea abies pendula*	2

2 SMALL TREES AND SHRUBS

	Zone
Red Jade Crabapple *Malus* Red Jade	3
Weeping Sargent Hemlock *Tsuga canadensis pendula*	3
Weeping Siberian Pea Shrub *Caragana arborescens pendula*	3
Forsythia *Forsythia suspensa*	4

F. *Columnar*

1 LARGE TREES

Port Orford Cypress *Chamaecyparis lawsonia erecta*	5
Arizona Cypress *Cupressus arizona*	6
Italian Cypress *Cupressus sempervirens stricta*	9
Columnar White Pine *Pinus strobus fastigiata*	4
Columnar Scotch Pine *Pinus sylvestris fastigiata*	4
Fastigiate varieties of	
Ginkgo	4
Maple	4
English Oak	5
Pyramidal Hornbeam *Carpinus betulus pyramidalis*	4

2 SMALLER TREES AND EVERGREENS

Van Eseltine Crab *Malus Van Eseltine*	3
Siberian Crab *Malus baccata columnaris*	3
Strathmore Crab *Malus Strathmore*	3
Tallhedge *Rhamnus frangula*	2
Chinese Juniper *Juniperus chinensis columnaris*	4
Irish Juniper *Juniperus hibernica*	5
Swiss Stone Pine *Pinus cembra pumila*	3
Irish Yew *Taxus baccata stricta*	5
Euonymus Sarcoxie *Euonymus Sarcoxie*	6

G. *Multiple or Low-branching Trunks*

Sometimes you will have to hunt for a multiple-trunked tree in a certain species. Redbud, for instance, often has a single stem. Birch trees are often planted in a clump. Nurserymen call them Clump Birch. Some of the plants listed under Picturesque Trees will have multiple trunks. Choose one carefully for the right spot.

Aralia sieboldi	8
Clump Birch Betula species	2
Crape Myrtle *Lagerstroemia indica*	7
Crabapples Malus species	3
Flowering Dogwood *Cornus florida*	6
Golden Shower *Cassia fistula*	9
Fringe Tree *Chionanthus virginica*	6

175

	Zone
Hawthorn Crataegus species	4
Amur Maple *Acer ginnala*	3
Saucer Magnolia *Magnolia soulangeana*	6
Madroña *Arbutus menziesii* (West Coast only)	9
Black Olive *Bucida buceras*	9
Olive *Olea europaea*	8
Oleander *Nerium oleander*	8
Photinia *Photinia fraseri*	7
Russian Olive *Elaeagnus angustifolia*	2
Redbud *Cercis canadensis*	4
Silk Tree *Albizzia julibrissin*	5
Serviceberry Amelanchier species	2
Smoke Tree *Cotinus obovatus*	5
Yellowwood *Cladrastis lutea*	5

H. *Globe or Oval-shaped*

1 TREES

Apple Malus species	3
Ash Fraxinus species	3
Beech *Fagus sylvatica*	4
Catalpa *Catalpa speciosa*	4
Chinaberry *Melia azedarach*	7
Hawthorn Crataegus species	3
Maple Acer species	3
Mountain Ash Sorbus species	3
Olive *Olea europea*	8
Pepper Tree *Schinus molle*	8
Canary Island Date Palm *Phoenix canariensis*	9
Carob Tree *Ceratonia siliqua*	9

2 SMALL TREES AND LARGE SHRUBS

India Laurel *Ficus retusa* var. *nitida*	9
Mountain Laurel *Kalmia latifolia*	4
Rhododendron Rhododendron species	4–6
Forsythia Forsythia species	5
Boxwood Buxus species	5–7
Barberry Berberis species	4
Beauty Bush *Kolkwitzia amabilis*	4
Hydrangea PeeGee *Hydrangea paniculata grandiflora*	4
Lilac Syringa species	2
Viburnum Viburnum species	3–7
Mugho Pine *Pinus mugho*	2
Weigela Weigela species	4
Honeysuckle Lonicera species	3

II TEXTURE

A. *Coarse*   *Zone*

	Zone
Castor Bean Annual, poisonous berries	3
Century Plant *Agave americana*	9
Leatherleaf Mahonia *Mahonia bealei*	6
Fatshedra *Fatshedra lizei*	9
Grape (vine) *Vitex* species	4
Dutchman's Pipe (vine) *Aristolochia durior*	4
Magnolia *Magnolia grandiflora*	7
Palms Palm species	8–10
Staghorn Sumac *Rhus typhina*	3
Yucca *Yucca filamentosa*	5
Oak-leaved Hydrangea *Hydrangea quercifolia*	5
David Viburnum *Viburnum davidi*	7
Hardy Bamboo *Sasa palmata*	5–6
Rhododendron *Rhododendron maximum*	3

B. *Fine*

	Zone
Japanese Barberry *Berberis thunbergi*	5
Heather *Calluna* species	4
Heath *Erica* species	4
Boxwood *Buxus* species	4–6
Dwarf Japanese Holly *Ilex crenata helleri*	6
Yaupon *Ilex vomitoria*	7
Hemlock *Tsuga canadensis*	3
Junipers *Juniperus* species	3–5
Teucrium *Teucrium chamaedrys*	5
Thunberg Spirea *Spiraea thunbergi*	4
Euonymus *Euonymus minimus* (vine)	6
Dwarf Arctic Willow *Salix purpurea nana*	2
Pachystima *Pachystima canbyi*	5

III GOOD FOUNDATION PLANTS

A. *Dwarf or Very Slow-growing*

I EVERGREEN

	Zone
Dwarf Abelia *Abelia grandiflora prostrata*	6
Boxwood Varder Valley *Buxus sempervirens* var. Varder Valley	5
Korean Boxwood *Buxus microphylla koreana*	4

177

	Zone
Red Elf Firethorn *Pyracantha* Red Elf	7
Dwarf Gardenia *Gardenia radicans*	8
Euonymus Jewel *Euonymus fortunei jewell*	5
Rose Daphne *Daphne cneorum*	4
Heller's Japanese Holly *Ilex crenata helleri*	5
Dwarf Chinese Holly *Ilex cornuta rotunda*	7
Dwarf Yaupon Holly *Ilex vomitoria nana*	7
Junipers, Prostrate species	
Procumbens	2
Andorra	4
Horizontalis	2
Chinensis sargenti	4
Dwarf Oregon Grape *Mahonia aquifolium compactum*	5
Malpighia *Malpighia coccigera*	10
Dwarf Nandina *Nandina domestica purpurea*	6
Pachistima *Pachistima canbyi*	5
Dwarf Rhododendron *Rhododendron myrtifolium*	6
Santolina *Santolina viridis* (green)	6
Santolina *Santolina chamaecyparissus* (gray)	6
Skimmia *Skimmia reevesiana*	7
India Hawthorn *Raphiolepsis indica* var. Enchantress	7
David Viburnum *Viburnum davidi*	7
Dwarf Japanese Yew *Taxus cuspidata nana*	4
Prostrate Japanese Yew *Taxus cuspidata prostrata*	4
Brown's Yew *Taxus media* Brown	4
Spreading English Yew *Taxus baccata repandens*	6

2 DECIDUOUS

	Zone
Crimson Pygmy Barberry *Berberis thunbergi* var. Crimson Pygmy	5
Warty Barberry *Berberis verruculosa*	6
Black Chokeberry *Aronia melanocarpa*	5
Rockspray Cotoneaster *Cotoneaster horizontalis*	5
Small-leaved Cotoneaster *Cotoneaster microphylla*	6
Cranberry Cotoneaster *Cotoneaster apiculata*	5
Dwarf Crape Myrtle *Lagerstroemia indica* var. Petite	6
Slender Deutzia *Deutzia gracilis*	5
Kelsey Red Twig Dogwood *Cornus stolenifera* var. Kelsey	4
Meyer Lilac *Syringa meyeri*	6
Dwarf Ninebark *Physocarpus opulifolius nana*	4
Dwarf Pomegranate *Punica granatum nana*	7
Dwarf Pea Shrub *Caragana pygmaea*	2

178

B. *Large Shrubs*

They do not always reach the full height and they can be trimmed. However, the more naturally they grow, the better.

I EVERGREENS	*Height*	*Zone*
Abelia *Abelia grandiflora*	5	5
Aucuba *Aucuba japonica* Shade	15	7
Andromeda *Pieris floribunda* Par. shade	6	4
Japanese Andromeda *Pieris japonica* Par. shade	9	5
Azaleas *Azalea species* Par. shade	4–6	6
Wintergreen Barberry *Berberis juliana*	6	6
Japanese Barberry *Berberis thunbergi*	6	5
Boxwood *Buxus sempervirens suffruticosa*	2–10	6
Cleyera *Cleyera japonica* Par. shade	10	7
Euonymus patens Euonymus kiautschovicus	8	6
Firethorn *Pyracantha lalandi*	6–10	6
Chinese Hibiscus *Hibiscus rosa sinensis*	8–10	8
India Hawthorn *Raphiolepis indica*	5	8
Yeddo Hawthorn *Raphiolepis umbellata ovata*	8	8
Inkberry *Ilex glabra compacta* Par. shade	6	4
Florida Jasmine *Jasminum floridum*	4	7
Laurel *Prunus laurocerasus*	6–20	7
Mountain Laurel *Kalmia latifolia* Par. shade	8	4
Mugho Pine *Pinus mugho*	8	2
Leucothoë *Leucothoë catesbyi* Shade	4	5
Myrtle *Myrtus communis*	5–10	8
Nandina *Nandina domestica*	8	6
Oregon Grape Holly *Mahonia aquifolia*	6	5
Osmanthus *Osmanthus species*	12	7–8
Pittosporum *Pittosporum tobira*	6–16	8
Pfitzer Juniper *Juniperus pfitzeriana*	7	5
Dwarf Pfitzer Juniper *Juniperus pfitzeriana* compacta	3	5
Podocarpus *Podocarpus macrophylla*	20	8
Rhododendron Rhododendron species Par. shade	6	5
Rosemary *Rosmarinus officinalis*	6	6
Yew Taxus species Shade	to 50	4
Very slow-growing and take shearing well		
Xylosma *Xylosma senticosum*	4–6	8
Yesterday-Today-and-Tomorrow *Brunfelsia latifolia*	4	9

179

	Height	Zone
Warminster Broom *Cytisus praecox*	6	5
Japanese Barberry Berberis species	6	5
Bayberry *Myrica pennsylvanica*	9	2
Red Twig Dogwood *Cornus stolonifera*	7	2
Winged Euonymus *Euonymus alatus*	10	3
Forsythia Forsythia species	9	5
Honeysuckle Lonicera species	9–20	2–5
Lilac Syringa species	6–20	3–5
Oak Leaf Hydrangea *Hydrangea quercifolia*	6	5
Ninebark *Physocarpus intermedia*	5	2
Regel's Privet *Ligustrum obtusifolium* var. *regeleanum*	6	5
Flowering Quince *Chaenomeles lagenaria*	6	4
Bridal Wreath *Spirea vanhouttei*	6	4
Burkwood Viburnum *Viburnum burkwoodi*	6	5
Doublefile Viburnum *Viburnum tomentosum* var. *mariesii*	9	4

IV PLANTS TO TRAIN AND TRIM

Azaleas Azalea species	5–8
Boxwood Buxus species	4–6
Bush Cherry *Eugenia myrtifolia*	10
Chinese Hibiscus *Hibiscus rosa sinensis*	10
Grewia *Grewia caffra*	10
Euonymus Euonymus species	6
False Cypress Chamaecyparis species	4
Flowering Dogwood *Cornus florida*	5
Firethorn *Pyracantha*	6
Japanese Holly *Ilex crenata*	7
Hemlock *Tsuga canadensis*	3
Hornbeam *Carpinus betulus*	4
Evergreen Magnolia *Magnolia grandiflora*	7
Loquat *Eriobotrya japonica*	10
Pfitzer Juniper *Juniperus pfitzeriana*	5
Privet Ligustrum species	5
Podocarpus *Podocarpus macrophylla*	7
Photinia *Photinia fraseri*	7
Rosemary *Rosmarinus officinalis*	8
Scotch Pine *Pinus sylvestris*	4
Yew Taxus species	2–5
Waxleaf Ligustrum *Ligustrum japonicum*	7

V PRICKLY SHRUBS

	Zone
Aralia Aralia species	3
Acanthopanax Acanthopanax species	4
Barberry	
Japanese *Berberis thunbergi*	5
Three Spine *B. tricanthophora*	5
Red *B. atropurpurea*	5
Wintergreen *B. juliana*	5
Korean *B. koreana*	5
Mentor *B. mentoris*	5
Cactus Species	7–10
Buckthorn *Rhamnus cathartica*	2
Carissa *Carissa grandiflora*	9
Chinese Holly *Ilex cornuta*	7
American Holly *Ilex opaca*	5
Firethorn *Pyracantha lalandi*	5
Flowering Quince Chaenomeles species	4
Thorny Russian Olive *Elaeagnus pungens*	7
Hardy Orange *Poncirus trifoliata*	6
Roses Rosa species	3

VI POLLUTION-TOLERANT PLANTS

Boxwood	Gingko
Camellia	Cotoneaster
Ash	Viburnum

MORE SENSITIVE BUT GOOD

Maple	Avocado
Alder	Sycamore
Hibiscus	Willow
Petunia	Rhododendron
Pine	Elm

INDEX

Ponds, 87, 108
Pools, 87; swimming, 67
Poplars: Lombardy, 17; Tulip, 11
Porches, 114
Port Royal Plantation, 89, 138
Prefabricated houses, 121–22
Prickly shrubs, 42, 181
Privet, 77; Regel's, 15, 158–59, 167
Pyracantha. *See* Firethorn

Quebec, 17

Railings, doorway, 78–80
Ranch-style house, 25
Redbud, 11
Rhododendrons, 17, 74, 78, 166
Rock gardens, 54, 137
Rocks, 38, 87
Roman (Palladian) architecture, 11, 13
Roof line, unbroken, 45–46
Rosedown plantation, 21
Roses, 3, 5, 21, 30, 71, 97, 169
Rural Gothic, 28–30

Sage (Salvia), 30, 96
St. Augustine, Florida, 21–22
Salem, Massachusetts, 6
Salt-box architecture, 2
Salvia (Sage), 30, 96
Santa Fe, New Mexico, 24
Santolina (Lavender Cotton), 67, 98, 101, 102
Scale, 163
Seclusion, 49
Sedums, 96, 100, 119–20
Shrubs, 166, 167–68 (*see also* Foliage; specific plants, types of architecture); and form, 155ff., 162, 173ff.; good foundation plants, 177–80; pollution-tolerant, 181; prickly, 181; and scale, 163; to train and trim, 180; and unity, 164ff.
Shutters, 69
Sites: distinctive, 83–90; grading, 123–38
Sky parks, 111–12
Slopes. *See* Sites; Steps
Small houses, 59. *See also* specific architecture, problems
Smokebush, 2
Southern homes, 1. *See also* specific plants, styles
Southernwood. *See* Artemisia
Southwest, 1, 23–25
Spain (and Spanish): and French Provincial, 19–20; style of architecture, 22–25, 35, 36, 76
Spindle Tree. *See* Euonymus
Split-level houses, 50–51, 132–33
Spruces, 163
Stachys. *See* Lamb's Ears
Steps, 150, 152, 153–54
Stocks, 96
Storage shed, 114

Sturbridge Village, 2
Suburban houses, 37–68
Sumac, Staghorn, 158
Swedes (the Swedish), 16, 18
Sycamores, 11

Teucrium, 67, 96, 102
Texture, 159–62, 177
Thyme (Thymus), 101, 102
Tidewater, Virginia, 11, 12
Town houses, 103–6
Tract houses, 38
Traditional houses, settings for, 1–36
Training and trimming, 180. *See also* Form; specific plants
Trees (*see also* Foliage; Sites; specific architecture, kinds of trees, problems, uses): and form, 155–59, 173–76; and grading, 123–25; pollution-tolerant, 181; and scale, 163; to train and trim, 180; and unity, 164–65
Trellises, 72, 73, 169
Tudor style, 6–10
Two-story houses (*see also* Traditional houses, settings for): formal, 55–56; at one end only, 52–54

Unity, 164–65

Van Cortlandt estate, 15
Vegetable gardening, 99, 120
Veronica, 96
Viburnum. *See* Cranberrybush
Victorian style, 28–30, 80
Vinca. *See* Periwinkle
Vines, 30, 132, 168, 169 (*see also* Trellises; specific plants); and doorways, 72, 73; and mobile homes, 117
Violets (Viola), 102
Virginia, 11, 12. *See also* specific places
Virginia Creeper, 30, 169
Virgin's Bower (Clematis), 169

Walks (paths), 141, 150–53 (*see also* Sites; Suburban houses); and dooryard gardens, 92, 101
Walls, 137, 154; dry, 125; retaining, 52, 56, 130–31ff.
Ward House, Salem, Massachusetts, 6
Washington, George, 26
Water, 87; drainage, 125–27; house on, 60–63
Weeping trees, 158, 174
Wells, tree, 125–27
Williamsburg, Colonial, 13, 77
Willows, Weeping, 158
Winter Creeper. *See* Euonymus
Wisteria, 30, 72, 169

Yaupon, 73, 102
Yews, 59, 78ff., 100, 101, 142, 162, 163; Japanese, 40, 69, 70; in traditional settings, 9, 13, 17, 25
Yuccas, 76